METRO LETTERS

A TYPEFACE FOR THE TWIN CITIES

A document of the “Typeface: Twin Cities” project, a component of the University of Minnesota Design Institute’s TWIN CITIES DESIGN CELEBRATION 2003, featuring the following invited typographers:

- PETER BIĽAK, Peter Biľak graphic design & typography (The Hague, The Netherlands)
- ERIK VAN BLOKLAND and JUST VAN ROSSUM, LettError (The Hague & Haarlem, The Netherlands)
- GILLES GAVILLET and DAVID RUST, Optimo (Geneva & Lausanne, Switzerland)
- SIBYLLE HAGMANN, Kontour (Houston, Texas)
- CONOR MANGAT, Inflection (Kentfield, California)
- ERIC OLSON, Process Type Foundry (Minneapolis & St. Paul, Minnesota)

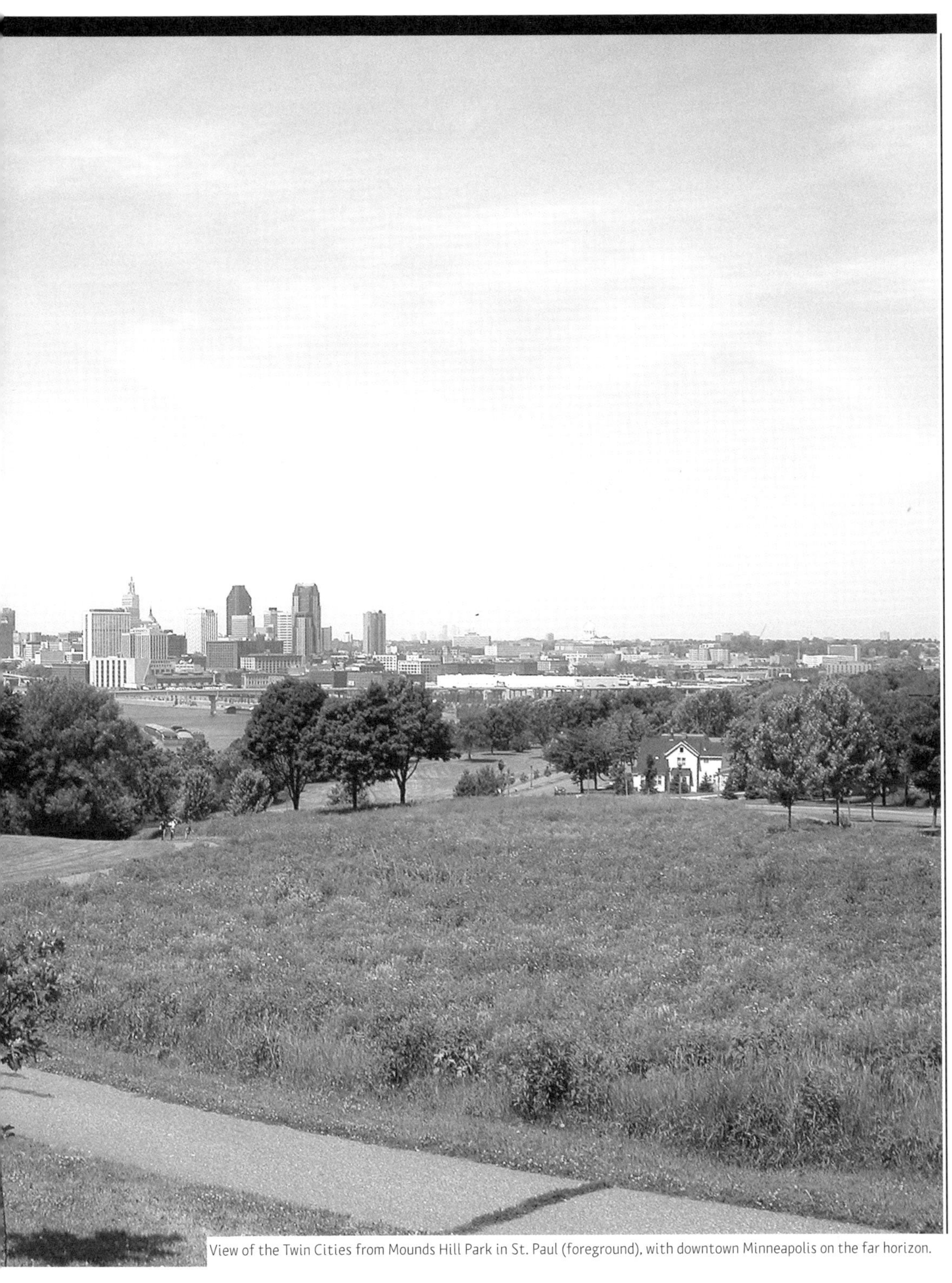

View of the Twin Cities from Mounds Hill Park in St. Paul (foreground), with downtown Minneapolis on the far horizon.

ST. PAUL

MINNEAPOLIS

thoroughfares

8
TWIN(S) IT IS:
THE BIRTH OF AN URBAN FONT
Janet Abrams

12
METRO LETTERS
A TYPEFACE FOR THE TWIN CITIES
Deborah Littlejohn

icons

14
MARKING THE PLACE
Gail Swanlund

24
TYPEFACE: TWIN CITIES
PROJECT DESCRIPTION

infrastructure

25
ERIC OLSON
PROPOSAL &
INTERVIEW
Process Type Foundry
Minneapolis, Minnesota

37
PETER BILÁK
PROPOSAL &
INTERVIEW
Peter Bil'ak, graphic design & typography
The Hague, The Netherlands

flow

49
CONOR MANGAT
PROPOSAL &
INTERVIEW
Inflection
Kentfield, California

63
GILLES GAVILLET &
DAVID RUST
PROPOSAL &
INTERVIEW
Optimo
Geneva & Lausanne, Switzerland

geography

71
SIBYLLE HAGMAN
PROPOSAL &
INTERVIEW
Kontour
Houston, Texax

83
ERIK VAN BLOKL
& JUST VAN ROSSU
PROPOSAL &
INTERVIEW
LettError
The Hague & Haar
The Netherlands

public space

97
TWIN TYPEFACE
PROCESS &
DEVELOPMENT

116
TYPE FOR THE
TWINS: A REVIEW
OF THE
TCDC PROPOSALS
Michael Worthing

134
INVITED JURY COMMENTS & CRITIQUE

160
CREDITS

152
ILLUSTRATED GLOSSARY

156
TYPEFACE SAMPLER

158
BIOGRAPHIES

competition

government

Compiled and illustrated by Eric Olson

views

arts & culture

METRO LETTERS

A TYPEFACE FOR THE TWIN CITIES

UNIVERSITY OF MINNESOTA
DESIGN INSTITUTE

TWIN(S) IT IS: BIRTH OF AN URBAN FONT

Janet Abrams

The "Typeface: Twin Cities" project started from a kind of dare. At a dinner in Spring 2002, following one of the lectures in the annual Insights graphic design series at the Walker Art Center, I murmured that it would be an interesting idea to commission a new typeface for a city, specifically, for the Twin Cities.

I had in mind an alternative approach to urban identity, something in contrast to typical city branding efforts that usually entail a heavily market-researched snappy slogan and a logo of simple and obvious appeal, drawing on some atavistic remnant of local industrial/sporting/geological mythology, slapped on to everything as a way to 'unify' (ie. simplify, banalize) the city's identity and make it visible and viable, at least iconographically, in the inter-urban competitive marketplace (for tourists, conventioneers, and corporate or "Creative Class" transplants).

I could imagine, instead, a more subtle form of identity: a typeface that would be used in city documents and literature and signage—something that could be quietly manifest in everything from utility bills to parking tickets, from transit timetables to community publications to street signs and "snow emergency"-type temporary notices. Something that would become part of the urban bloodstream.

I also had fresh in memory the experience of arriving in Minneapolis a little over a year earlier, and finding myself just too late to become usefully involved in the design of the graphics for the city's (still) forthcoming Light Rail Transit system—alas, it had seemed such a ripe opportunity for the city to rethink itself visually and as a shared public space. (The LRT signage, though clean and legible, will utilize existing fonts, and so will break no new ground typographically).

Having grown up in London, traveling the Tube every day throughout high school, I was and remain imbued with the simple grandeur of the typeface designed by Edward Johnston in 1916 as the system font for the London Underground. This serviceable sans serif has weathered the decades and transition to the digital typography era; a signifier of modernity (at the time of its creation), by now it is an historic artifact, a typographic fossil, patina'd with memory (like the velveteen pile of the Tube seats' upholstery) accrued over long years of passenger use.

With these references in mind, I was surprised by the vehement response to my modest proposal at that Insights dinner.

To implement such a font would be a kind of top-down imposition, bordering on visual fascism, pronounced one of my fellow diners (who knows who he is, but shall remain nameless). How could such a typeface not become autocratic, dictatorial? Indeed, he demanded to know, how could such a project avoid being just another version of the mindless branding exercises so ubiquitous in corporate America, transferred to the realm of public service?

That was enough. I was determined to try and find out.

Shortly after that dinner, back at the Design Institute, while we were in the early stages of defining this year's Twin Cities Design Celebration, I gingerly broached the idea of commissioning a typeface for the Twin Cities as a kind of research experiment on the relationship between typography and urban identity—a form of cultural mapping (a topic emerging as the connective theme of the TCDC).

The response at base camp was a lot more enthusiastic. Deborah Littlejohn, then recently arrived as the DI's resident Design Fellow (responsible for all DI graphic production and the majority of its editorial design too) seized on the project and ran with it. As Project Manager for "Typeface: Twin Cities," Deb shaped my crude kernel of an idea into a succinct yet comprehensive brief, helped assemble the shortlist of typographers to be invited to take part in the project's conceptual first phase, and then not only managed the competition and subsequent jury process, but also served as principal liaison with the selected typographers, Erik van Blokland and Just van Rossum, in the Netherlands, throughout the process of full font development (including, during the competition phase, vouchsafing to U.S. Customs and Immigration that the package being Fed Ex'd to the DI from a certain LettError was of no threat to Homeland Security!).

Deb then went to Europe to interview the three invited designers based there, and has somehow developed this book, *Metro Letters*, amidst production of three Knowledge Maps, the RFP for the new TCDC Knowledge Maps, and (with Assistant Design Fellow Eric Olson) the creation of the Twin Cities Design Celebration identity. Then there are the "Chocoletters"—the limited edition of *Twin* which we're having made in honor of the Dutch tradition of casting letters in chocolate.

The chosen font, *Twin*, is so mutable and so varied in its (eventual family of ten) print alphabets, even before we get to the online "live and reactive" version, that it fulfills the dream of a typeface capable of representing a city's diverse denizens—long-standing as well as recent residents, new immigrants and temporary tourists—in all their idiosyncrasies and constant evolutions. And the face of Minneapolis and St. Paul is certainly changing: into the Scandinavian/German heartland, thousands of new citizens have recently arrived from Ethiopia, Eritrea and Somalia, as well as a large Hmong community, enlivening the cities with their cultures, musical and culinary traditions, languages and dress. North meets South: the grey-blue mirror-tint of downtown's skyscraper gridscape never looks so gorgeous as when contrasted by the desert colors of a knot of East African women, dressed respectfully in their flowing full-length robes.

Can a typeface effectively represent a city, or communicate what's unique about a particular place? Maybe. Maybe not. We knew we didn't want something literal, and though all six proposals were provocative (as you will read in the jury critique section) and took strikingly different approaches to this core question, it was the risk-factor in the LettError proposal that captured our imagination—as well as the immediate friendliness (the almost runic, Celtic wink) exuded by even the rudimentary font, on their initial concept boards. One juror described himself as 'scared' by their proposal. Would it, *could* it work?

The possible permutations of what would eventually be named *Twin* seemed almost too plentiful to contemplate. The font concept came bundled with the prospect of something called the "Panchromatic Hybrid Style Alternator" which, at the time, we couldn't entirely fathom: a tongue-in-cheek Heath Robinson-esque joke, we guessed, though it turned out to be no such thing—instead, a rather sophisticated piece of randomizing software.

Thus capable of self-selecting from among multiple variants of individual letters within a single word, or within a body of text, *Twin* proposes that identity need not mean identical—that we can share common "family" characteristics, display an underlying relatedness, while nevertheless maintaining our individual uniqueness and distinctive attributes, one from the other. What better metaphor for a city?

And as if this was not already innovative enough, with its Internet-enabled edition, *Twin* is capable of morphing on-the-fly in response to actual changing urban conditions, echoing the mood and climate of the city in its own outlines, its shifting wardrobe of serifs, pig-tail curlicues and ladder-back letterforms. Typeface as weather-vane. Of course, *Twin* could be connected to data from *any* city, but the fact is that this experiment is being tried for the first time here, in Minneapolis and St. Paul.

Shortly after their selection, the LettError partners admitted that they'd conceived of a dynamically data-driven font a decade ago, but it had taken until now for the technology to make it feasible. And it had taken this Design Institute commission to provide the opportunity to test their hypothesis and make it happen.

For this is certainly one of our goals at the DI: to enable the most gifted young designers to develop new ideas, new prototypes, to create the next significant work in their portfolio. The Design Institute has, perhaps unfashionably, defined design for the public realm as its focus of attention. It aims to stand in relation to professional design discourse as independent film stands in relation to Hollywood production. To move the practices of design along, and develop truly path-breaking propositions, we need to undertake practical experiments, in an atmosphere of daring, risk, and initiative. The "Typeface: Twin Cities" project is one such venture.

Will *Twin* become adopted as the "home font" of Minneapolis and St. Paul, recognizable both here and far as "our" typeface? We'd like to think so, and scattered throughout this book, you'll find some "after" images, shots of generic city graphics, doctored by Deb Littlejohn to demonstrate how *Twin* might look *in situ*.

As this book goes to press, the Greater Minneapolis Convention and Visitors' Association has just released the findings of its year-long research into the "image" of Minneapolis (and St. Paul), and the results suggest that the time has come for a new, more sophisticated expression of the city's identity—both for business visitors, and for those of us whose experience of place unfolds over more than the proverbial "Three Perfect Days" beloved of in-flight magazines.

Though there's no guarantee that a project hatched as a conceptual exercise within a university research institute will gain purchase outside the Ivory Tower, we stand by the possibility that an idea like this could 'catch light', if the typeface became seeded into the community as a tool for multiple graphic articulations—used in all its infinite acrobatics, from *Formal* to *Weird*, depending on the user and the context.

Our thanks are due to the citizens of Minnesota, who support the DI through the State Legislature's funding for this Strategic Academic Initiative at the University of Minnesota, and to Target Corporation, for its generous gift to the DI, which we have parlayed into several projects, including the 2002 and 2003 Design Camp for teens and the five major components of the Twin Cities Design Celebration 2003. We also gratefully acknowledge additional support for "Typeface: Twin Cities" from the Mondriaan Foundation, Amsterdam, and the Consulate General of the Netherlands in New York.

Can a typeface truly represent a city? Read on, and decide. And, to adapt a phrase from round these parts:

"GO TWIN!"

METRO LETTERS: A TYPEFACE FOR THE TWIN CITIES

Deborah Littlejohn

In July 2002, the University of Minnesota Design Institute invited several national and international type design studios to propose a new typeface for its Twin Cities Design Celebration (TCDC), the DI's major upcoming program for 2003. Because the chosen typeface would be used for public events, Fellows' projects and Design Institute publications whose subject matter related to the Twin Cities of Minneapolis and St. Paul, we asked that the character of these adjacent cities be reflected in the designers' concepts—in the use of the typeface, in the process of its construction, or in its formulating concepts. The chosen typeface, therefore, would function not so much to brand the cities themselves, but to brand the TCDC and in doing so, engage the public's awareness and appreciation of design and typography in the city.

Just as other designed artifacts (architecture, furniture, fashion) have the ability to touch us beyond their utilitarian value, so too can letterforms establish meaning in a way that cannot be measured by function alone. In composing the "Typeface: Twin Cities" brief for the half dozen studios that responded to our invitation, we embraced the conviction that typography has an aesthetic worth in its own right—that it does more than merely serve the practical purpose of communicating information (though legibility *is* one of its primary attributes).

In mid-September 2002, six concepts (plus a second entry from Peter Bil'ak) arrived at the Design Institute's offices. These concepts provoked fascinating discussions, which took place in October among an assembled expert panel of Twin Cities-based designers and critics and one local government official, and are duly included in this book.

Based on these deliberations and some subsequent debate within the Design Institute about our needs and ambitions for the typeface, we settled on the concept submitted by Erik van Blokland and Just van Rossum of LettError, the renowned Netherlands-based type design studio—not only because it was a warm, multi-faceted, well-drawn font (as were the other five studios' submissions), but because of the intriguing comments made by our panelists about how bold LettError's approach was, and how dangerously unpredictable the results might be.

After several months of design development, by June 2003 our new typeface, *Twin*, was ready for use in TCDC print materials, advertisements, systems, chocolate letters and in this book, *Metro Letters*, which documents the "Typeface: Twin Cities" selection process.

As the pages of *Metro Letters* reveal, the Design Institute's hypothetical question: "Can a typeface communicate the special character of a city?" was met with a surprising mix of answers: "No, but then...," "I don't know, however...," and "Perhaps, yet not without..." Happily, although the designers' responses were in many cases equivocal, their conceptual and formal proposals (and the jury's discussions of them) did not categorically refute our initial question, either. During the invited critique sessions, the seed was sown of an idea that would eventually grow into a "live and reactive" online version of the selected typeface—an idea that, to our knowledge, has not been developed before.

In spite of their difficulties with our generative question, all six type design studios produced concepts that were innovative, enthusiastic, and likely to engage the attention and curiosity of the people of the Twin Cities, and of designers everywhere.

Conceptual exercises and the messy process of research and development are essential aspects of design that are often overlooked when the shiny new "thing" has been brought to life in its final form. Indeed, these early processes, particularly as practiced in graphic design, are rarely granted the reflection and critique they deserve — much less a documentation that goes beyond the formulaic, pictorial narratives of most contemporary graphic design and typography publications.

It is for this reason that we decided to expose the "behind the scenes" process of the "Typeface: Twin Cities" project: how the Design Institute formulated, described, chose and finally (with a great deal of work by Erik and Just!) brought to life our new typeface. We present this publication in the hope that it will provide further food for thought on the question of whether a typeface can represent what is truly special about a city.

MARKING THE PLACE

Gail Swanlund

"If you don't get your type warm it will be just a smooth, commonplace, third-rate piece of good machine technique—no use at all for setting down warm human ideas—just a box full of rivets . . . I'd like to make it warm—so full of blood and personality that it would jump at you."
—*W.A. Dwiggins,* Emblems and Electra, 1935.

Grizzly bears, when moved long distances from their native territory, will lumber all the way back home. No one really knows how they find their way back. Perhaps the bear heeds an internal navigational system, or follows clues like a particular slant of the sun's rays, or recognizes a series of strategic marks clawed into the bark of trees. For us humans, too, the language of elements that makes up a sense of place is simultaneously elusive while utterly familiar.

Twelve-thousand years ago, the Wisconsin glacier—the massive layer of ice and rock that once buried and scoured the expanse of land where the twin cities of Minneapolis and St. Paul now flourish—began to retreat for the last time. Where the ice had been, beavers the size of black bears waddled and splashed in the melt of future Minneapolis lakes. Glacial Lake Agassiz, formed by run-off from the final receding lobe of ice, covered most of not-yet Minnesota. Thousands of years of water were sent rushing southward to carve out river beds, pool into numerous lakes and sink into peat bogs. Rich Agassiz deposits created a velvety fragrant dirt, gentle hills and prairies, and deeply folded valleys. Boulders that had been embedded in the ice or carried by the water, abruptly appeared sitting in the middle of the wide flat plains.

As the climate warmed, the river bluffs at the confluence of the Mississippi and the Minnesota Rivers, where the Twin Cities would one day take root, grew into what is known as a Temperate Eastern Broadleaf Zone. Hardwoods, brushes and grasses began to prosper. Humans arrived, first a nomadic people who hunted in the area. Later, permanent seasonal villages sprang up around the cultivation of wild rice from lakes and streams. Ice fishing, tobogganing, and hockey-like games were popular with the Dakota and Ojibwe long before French explorers, fur traders, and missionaries traveled the waterways of the state. An ever-widening stream of immigrants and homesteaders, mostly from Northern Europe, began to arrive, dig in sod homes, uproot trees and plant crops. In 1858 Minnesota became the thirty-second state.

Minneapolis and St. Paul resemble conjoined twins. Partially separated by the Mississippi River, the cities still share a hip and a bladder: the limestone gorge of the Mississippi runs right through Minneapolis, and turning east, it slices the capital city St. Paul in two. The Western most city is named by stitching the Dakota word, *minne*, meaning "water," to the Greek suffix for "city," *polis*. The State capital, initially called "Pig's Eye" after an industrious bootlegging resident who conducted business from the caves along the Mississippi, has been renamed a more respectable-sounding "St. Paul."

An outsider would have difficulty telling the twins apart, but to those who dwell here, they are wildly different. One city takes up a little more room than the other. One has built itself into bluffs with wide views of the river valley. One is more cosmopolitan, the other has preserved its historical buildings. Minneapolis restricts skyscrapers to 51 stories, St. Paul does not. The twins often speak in unison, with rounded 'O's' that sound like wind blowing across a pop bottle. A body of water is within strolling distance of every resident; access to lakes and rivers is regarded as essential and private ownership of a beach is unthinkable. Contrary to popular misconceptions perpetuated by folksy radio shows, the cities are diverse, warmly welcoming immigrants from all over the globe.

The soil in which the Twin Cities are rooted is fertile in every sense. The two share a spectacular world-class collection of art and orchestras—chamber and full—innovative industry and technology, and more educational institutions per square inch than any other city in the world. A conspicuous display of wealth is considered bad manners. Foundations open-handedly endow the arts. Politics are lively and progressive; engaged personal participation is a given. Bread and beer and Scotch tape are long-time, formidable industries. Farms within the metro area's city limits produce the sweetest strawberries anywhere. Leisurely approaching thunderstorms push sparrows and the scent of cut grass ahead in their course. The residents of these cities have no need for vitamins, because living in Minnesota is good enough for you already.

◎◎◎◎

A sense of place is evoked and defined by these influential factors: by the people with whom one is in contact; by the location, its geography, mobility and commerce; and by each individual's personal experiences there. But in the case of the Twin Cities, let's say that the last determining component is the weather.

Weather is a force that frames the experience of those who live in the midwest. In 1886, a reporter from New York wrote that St. Paul was "unfit for human habitation." Severe storms and extreme variations in temperature year-round—a range of 170 degrees has been officially recorded—are accepted as routine, much as the certainty that the sun will rise tomorrow. Epic blizzards move in without much warning. The morning of the famous Armistice Day Blizzard of 1940 began warmly and mildly then swiftly turned into a whiteout that dropped 17 inches of snow on the Twin Cities with drifts up to 20 feet deep. Duck hunters were caught unawares; in shirtsleeves they froze to death, shotguns in hand, when they couldn't make their way back. In sub-zero temperatures, exposed flesh freezes in a few minutes, nostril membranes freeze brittle and eyes ice shut. When I was an orderly in a hospital, a man wearing just shorts for a sub-zero run arrived at the E.R. I saw his skin drop from his thighs in tattered hunks. And summer temperatures too can be erratic: in June the temperature in the Twin Cities has been known to drop below freezing and has also hit a high of 114. Pragmatism and a certain sense of humor are essential for survival here. Nearly the entire evening news is devoted to forecast and weather statistics and for Minnesotans, the narration of the weather report is the soundtrack to daily life.

Going to Minneapolis and St. Paul, Minnesota

1. Characters from Frank Heine's *Remedy*, (1991), *Emigre*, Inc.

◎◎◎◎

An alphabet is comprised of twenty-six or so letterforms that stand in as mnemonic devices for a set of vocalizations. In English, despite regional variations in enunciation, we pretty much all agree how to sound out these letters. The basic letterforms are just skeletons until the type designer adds flesh and shapes their gesture. With modularity and rigor, the type designer determines the plumpness or curvature of a stroke, the tension of the connective tissue that binds a serif to a stem, and the gravity of the letter sitting on the baseline. These are the physical characteristics that are suggestive of a typeface's disposition towards a particular temperament and personality. See *Emigre's* sunny *Remedy* as an example: 'O's' are bouncy spirals, and 'S's' sprout cheerful hair (FIGURE 1). So, let's consider: could a typeface be engineered with sense-of-place somehow sewn in, custom-tailored for the Twin

Cities, fortified and somehow representative of culture, geography and weather?

As the LettErrorists have said, "The streets and buildings don't care for one typeface or the other." The buildings may be unimpressed, but Matthew Carter provided snap-on serifs for *Walker*, a typeface he designed for the Walker Art Center, and this device *does* bring to mind the skyways that conjoin the business buildings in both downtown Minneapolis and St. Paul (SEE P. 120). And it's enchanting to imagine that he had that in mind. But in fact, Carter saw his letterforms "...rather like store window mannequins with good bone structure on which to hang many kinds of clothing," not buildings connected by skywalks at all. Typographer and designer Edward Fella says his typeface *Outwest (on a 15 Degree Ellipse)* is inspired by the romantic vernacular of Hollywood's mythological West. *Outwest* alludes to Westerns, to signs, cattle brands, and the lonesome saguaro cactus (FIGURE 2). A cowboy hat doubles for the bullet symbol and the cartoony drawing style is akin to Disney's Mickey Mouse, both in terms of the Mouse himself and its goofy playfulness. The optimism of the Golden Dream (or wistful longing and disillusionment) is slyly insinuated by the typeface's weights, *Half-Full* and *Half-Empty*. Still, *Outwest* doesn't lock down "the West." "The way to show 'place' is to literally depict it," says Fella, "and then sit down and draw the particulars."

Oh! Give me a home
Outwest Half-Full
where the buffalo
roam • Where the
Outwest Half-Empty
deer and the antelope
play...

2. Characters from Ed Fella's *Outwest (on a 15 Degree Ellipse)*, (1993), showing the two variations *Outwest Half-Full* and *Outwest Half-Empty*, *Emigre*, Inc.

Some linguists theorize that from birth we carry the universal structure of language in our gray matter. With visual language, we learn to identify what each letter represents. Letters are strung together to make linguistic sense, letters are made into words and words into sentences. The interpretation of visual language—the "read" that we fasten together in our heads—is very slippery, in no way fixed or universal.

Consider blackletter and its intimate associations with nationalism and the Third Reich—the party's embrace and later rejection of it: because of that identification, ensuing relationships with the letterforms are forever tainted. But, in spite of Nazi baggage, other connotations still instantly spring to mind: storybooks, German beer labels, diplomas, gang turf marking, bibles, tombstones, newspaper mastheads and heavy metal. Skinheads deploy letterforms shared with rustic ski resort signage and retro-Disneyland. No other typeface is as evocative, at once connoting sweeping heroism and imperialism, disaffection and intolerance, while also conjuring notions as sweet and dependable as a cup of cocoa.

◎◎◎◎

It's 1898 in Kensington, Minnesota. Olof Ohman, an unschooled farmer, is grubbing a living on his swampy farmland. One drizzly Fall afternoon, Ohman and his son discover a tombstone-sized slab of graywacke—a regional hard glacial sandstone—tangled in the roots of an aspen that they are pulling. The stone is face down and when righted, Ohman discovers unfamiliar letters carved into the face and edge of the slab. The strokes of the inscribed characters are pointy, yet neat and precise, chiseled into the stone with straight cuts. After being carried into town, the stone is roped to the bed of a horse cart and transported to the University of Minnesota to be examined by O. J. Breda, a professor of Scandinavian history and skeptic. Breda identifies the letterforms as runes and translates the inscription. It reads,

> *"(We are) 8 Goths and 22 Norwegians on (an) exploration-journey from Vinland over the West. We had camp by 2 skerries, one days-journey north from this stone. We were (out) and fished one day. After we come home (we) found 10 (of our) men red with blood and dead. AV(e) M(aria) Save us from evil. (We) have 10 of our party by the sea to look after our ship(s?) 14 days-journey from this island. Year 1362"* (FIGURE 3).

Breda is not impressed. For one thing, he finds the stone's mish-mash of Swedish and Norwegian language troubling and the letterforms inconsistent with other medieval runic alphabets (known as *futharks*). He also believes the timetable described in the inscription to be implausible, that 14 days would have been insufficient for the expedition team to have paddled and portaged from the Hudson Bay, down the Nelson River, the Red River, and to have hiked in over 40 miles to Ohman's sloggy farm.

Word of the runestone travels and scholars in Chicago request to examine the monument up close. Breda packs it up and ships it via train eastward. After a bumpy ride, the stone is scrubbed, probed, chipped and cut into, letterforms re-scribed, tested with various caustic chemicals, and the stone is declared a hoax. It is returned to Ohman;

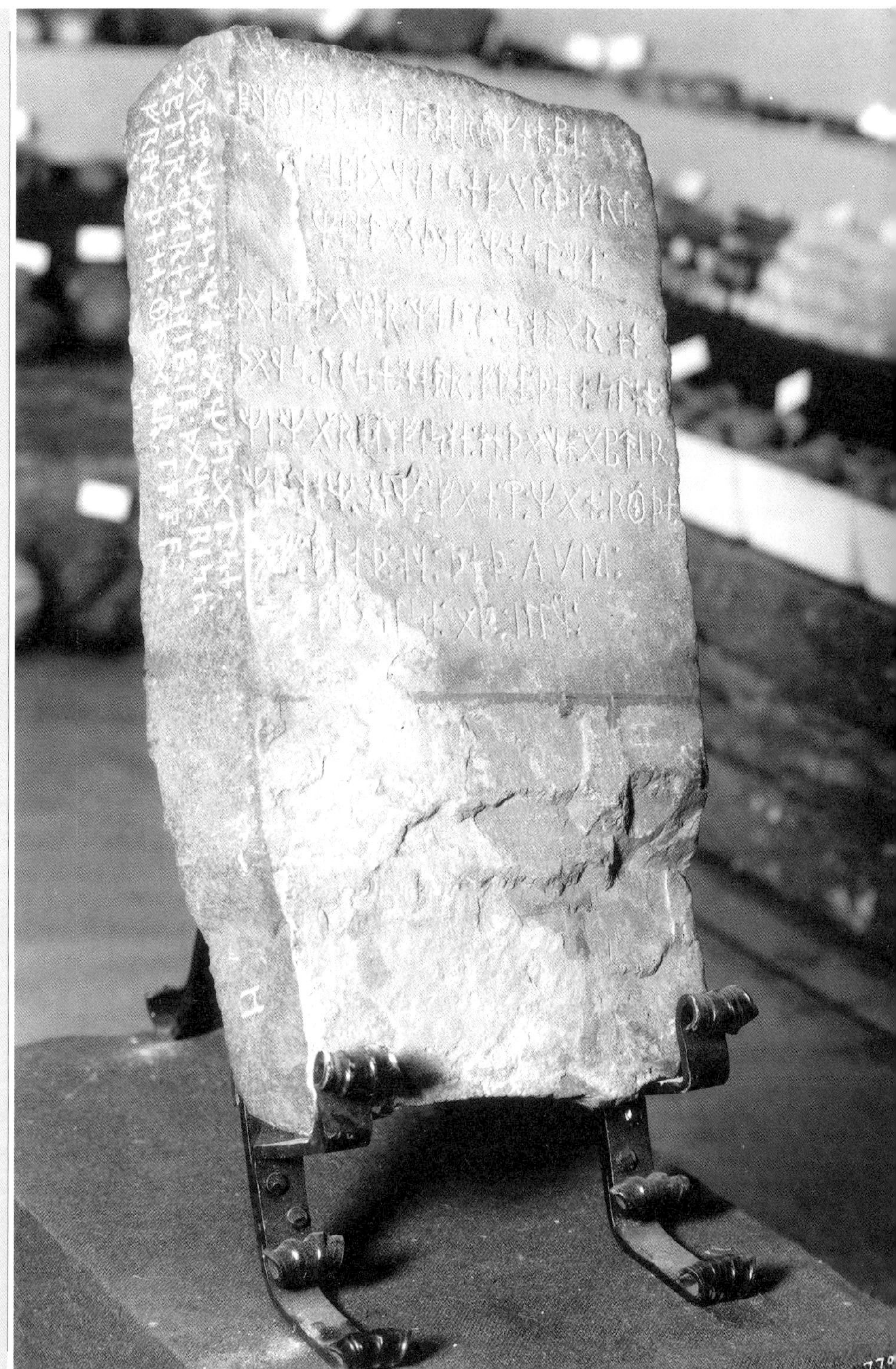

GAIL SWANLUND

he is happy to see the slab again because it is the perfect size for a granary stoop. The taciturn farmer is said by his neighbors to be honest and trustworthy. Surely that should be enough to prove the runic inscription's sincerity: this is the highest compliment a Minnesotan can be paid.

Over the next century, the debate over the stone periodically revives. Tidbits of information emerge: scholars believe four chisels were used to incise the letterforms, the tools kept sharp by a very hot fire. A petrographic team cores out a rock plug to determine whether discoloration on the back is due to the roots of the tree Ohman allegedly chopped away from the stone; that story is deemed plausible.

The argument for authenticity comes to rest on hotly disputed linguistic and typographic issues. In question is whether certain marks, grammar, and spelling rendered on the stone are consistent with written practice of the 14th century. Among numerous typographic spars, a stray apostrophe gouged between the 'AV' and 'M' creates an abbreviation that may or may not be datable to 1362. Problematic too, in addition to other grammatical discrepancies, is that the inscribed word, *opdagelse*, or "discovery," is in modern usage and not documented in other medieval runic evidence.

3. The Kensington Runestone on display, location unknown. September 7, 1929. Photo by Norton & Peel, Minnesota Historical Society.

Accusations of "lack of intellectual rigor" are flung back and forth across the ocean. Formerly polite academic arguments verge on pugilism. In 1951, Erik Moltke, the official Runologist of the Danish National Museum, resolutely dismisses the stone because of the appearance of an "invented" letterform in the word *sklar*, [trans. either "skerries" or "shelters," still in dispute]. This letterform would be a modern equivalent of a 'J', not the hard German 'J', but a silky enunciation closer to an 'L'. The debate is revived again when it is found that the disputed letterform is shared with a 14th century manuscript of the Danish realm, *AM 28 8vo*, also known as *Codex Runicus*, that defines the law concerning the fine a man will pay for wounding another man. It's entirely possible that Ohman may have been acquainted with popular Swedish runic publications of the day, but this J-rune, as well as a number of other alphabetic forms used in the inscription, are not cataloged by scholars until a number of year after the stone's unearthing. And then, there are unconfirmed rumors of deathbed confessions that implicate Ohman and neighboring farmers.

Ultimately, the stone's veracity is not as interesting as the public interest it piques. The loveliness of the inscription on the Kensington Runestone can be found in the ideas and the associations we attach to it, at the very instant the mystery resonates in the imagination and follows the watery trail that leads from the hole where the stone was unearthed, across the sea of prairie grass, up the Red River, a series of lakes, the Nelson River, Hudson Bay, and back across the ocean.

Incongruously, at the bottom of the *Codex Runicus*, a straightforward document of law, are the words to a song with musical notation, a tune familiar to Danes as the interval signal used on Danish radio:

> DRØMDE MIK EN DRØM I NAT, UM SILKI OK ÆRLIK PÆL
> (I dreamt a dream last night, of silk and fine fur).

Human sensibilities determine the handling of meaning, which is only tenuously attached to reality. For only a brief moment do we own what we make and what it is intended to mean. Once it is released from our hands, its use and interpretation belong to the world at large, its significance thrives—and may change—elsewhere.

◎◎◎◎

Aurora borealis may be viewed on the outskirts of the Twin Cities on crisp winter nights, sometimes as early as September. The waving curtains of light materialize and vanish in shimmering cycles, obscure and faint and then suddenly distinct, if only for a split second. When viewing northern lights, it is best to look obliquely, from the corner of the eyes, where the rods and cones are most receptive to dim light.

The residents of Minneapolis and St. Paul pride themselves not only on integrity and practicality, but on innovation and adventurous thought. And so, an intellectual activity, like the introduction and utilization of a new typeface designed exclusively for the Twin Cities Design Celebration, would naturally be welcomed enthusiastically by the residents of these two cities. The question of whether any typeface could be truly representative of a diverse citizenry, weather and rolling plains, and whether a language of letterforms can convey a sense of place through unique and identifiable characteristics, can be answered not by approaching directly, but only by gazing askance, taking its measure through our peripheral vision.

PROJECT DESCRIPTION & TYPOGRAPHERS' INTERVIEWS

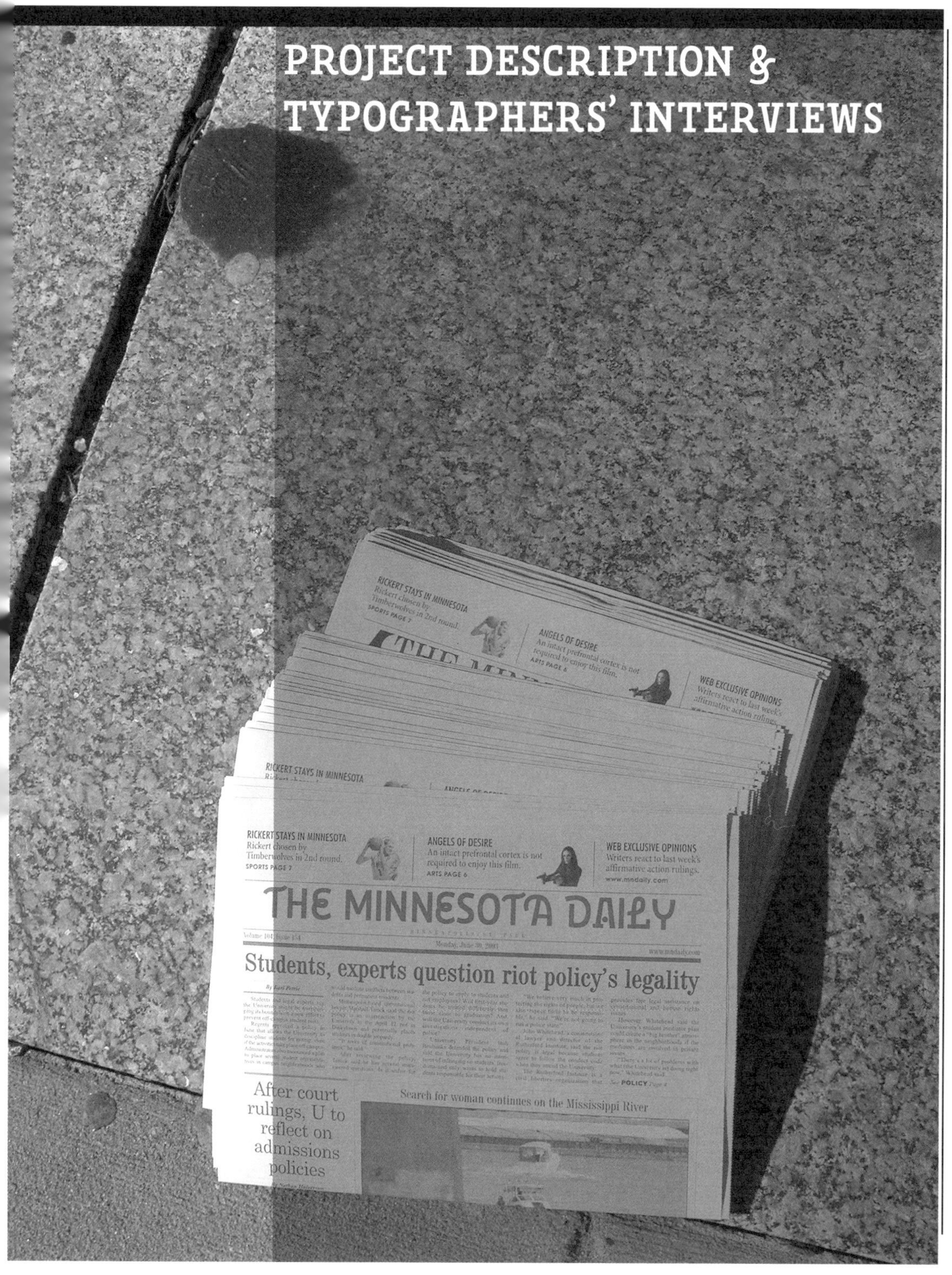

TYPEFACE: TWIN CITIES Request for Proposals

Can a typeface communicate the characteristics of a city?

PROPOSITION

The University of Minnesota Design Institute wishes to commission from talented typographers concepts for a new typeface for use in our Twin Cities Design Celebration 2003 (TCDC).

PRETEXT

The selected typeface will be showcased in the TCDC, and should somehow express the character of the Twin Cities of Minneapolis and St. Paul—two sister cities which, in 2003 and beyond, will unveil some of America's most interesting architecture and urban design. The typeface will be used in the collateral material produced by the Design Institute to brand the TCDC—and to promote the Twin Cities nationally and internationally. The TCDC is an excellent opportunity for the Twin Cities to celebrate its culture(s) and to bring out the pride Minnesotans have in their two major cities. This typeface will not be used so much to brand the cities themselves, but to brand a festival that raises people's awareness of Twin Cities typography and design. The type/mark should be applicable as an identity in its most basic form "TCDC 2003" but could expand to include other signatures or typographic lock-ups, according to the concept.

PLAN

The typeface should be considered in a variety of formats including: promotional print material, newsletters, magazines, stationery, posters, postcards, signage and wayfinding systems related to outdoor events, billboards, broadcast, web, etc.

PROMOTION

The Design Institute will use each studio's proposal as a project for inclusion in the TCDC. Additionally, the DI will feature all participants in a publication documenting the Typeface: Twin Cities development process, with interviews and images featuring each designer's work. Possible public events that may be scheduled around this project include lectures, symposia, and student critique sessions.

PRESENCE

The DI is also interested in seeking other possible applications, both for and beyond the TCDC, including:

- wayfinding and signage that link Twin Cities public transit with cultural venues and activities
- use in other public/civic applications and/or systems
- generating a TCDC type-mark or logotype

PAYMENT

Each designer will receive an initial honorarium to produce concepts (not a complete font initially) for Phase One submissions, due September 16, 2002. We will appoint a designer in early October who will receive an additional development fee to bring the font to completion for use in early 2003.

ERIC OLSON
PROCESS TYPE FOUNDRY
MINNEAPOLIS, MINNESOTA

Interviewed in Minneapolis by Deborah Littlejohn

March 5, 2003

"Ultimately, the typeface should be conceptually derived or serve as support for the graphic design of the [TCDC] project."

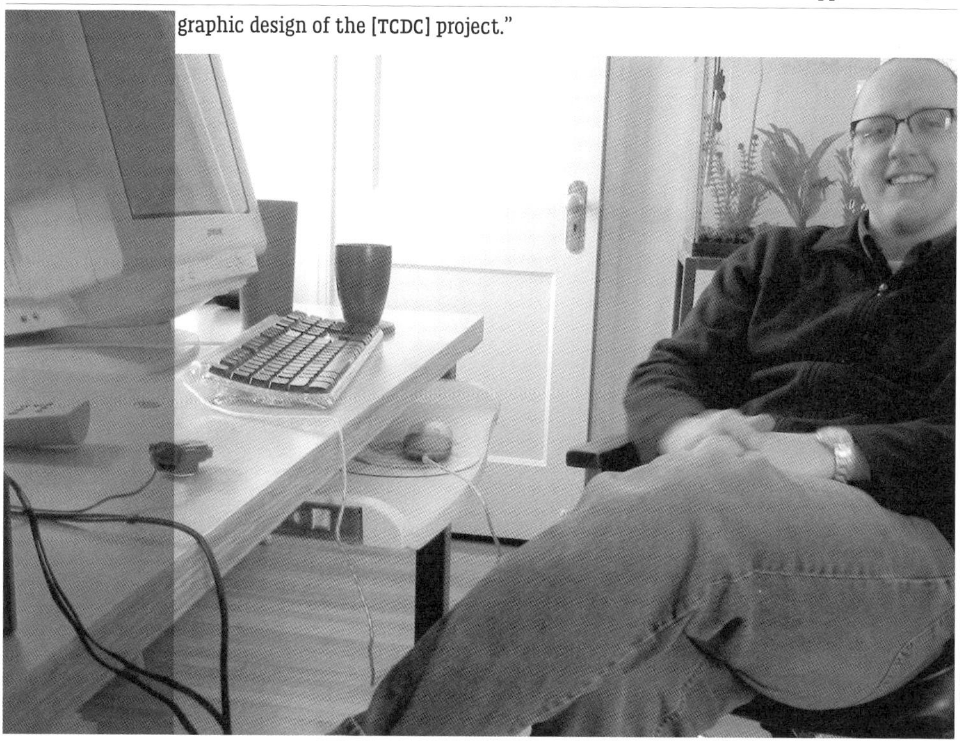

TWIN CITIES DESIGN 2003

Eric Olson: TCDC typeface proposal, board 1.

Eric Olson: TCDC typeface proposal, board 2.

CE
403
MN
DI

NEW ARCHITECTURE NOW
SATELLITE NAVIGATION CAN BE USED FOR SIMPLE SURVEYING
DOCUMENTATION MAP
TASKS SUCH AS DEFINING A PROPERTY LINE OR FOR
URBAN CENTERS
COMPLEX OPERATIONS LIKE BUILDING SPECS
MINNEAPOLIS
AND STEEP GRADE CELL LINE TRAPS
2 CITIES

Eric Olson: TCDC typeface proposal, board 3.

DEBORAH LITTLEJOHN: **You are originally from Minneapolis, you studied design at the University of Minnesota in St. Paul, and now you've set up Process Type Foundry back again in Minneapolis. What impact has the ambience of the Twin Cities had on your approach to design?**
ERIC OLSON: Being native has likely influenced me in ways I'm unaware of, but the Minneapolis design scene *per se* has had little effect on me. I've never worked in a commercial design or advertising studio. However, there is a small, but talented group of designers working in the cultural sector here who have influenced me greatly. While I was in college, I lived near the Walker Art Center. Looking back, maybe that rubbed off on me. After graduation, my first jobs were with non-profit art galleries, and then later as a full-time designer for the Walker.

What year did you graduate from the U of M?
1999.

Oh, that's so recent! *{laughs}*
It is. But the Walker forced me to forget all of it! In a way, I erased everything that I had done up to that point. It was a completely new situation for me that rearranged my approach to design in a very healthy way. So if there's a Minneapolis influence on me, it's the Walker.

What led you to become a typographer?
Several things, but most important, in the mid-Nineties there was a great deal of optimism surrounding type design. For young students like myself, free issues of *Emigre* magazine were fuel. *Emigre* made type design seem approachable and completely possible. As a gift, my boss at the University's Student Union purchased a copy of Fontographer for me. After that, I was on my way.

At first, I designed type out of an immediate need. For my job, I was making roughly a poster a day. After a few months, I couldn't bear the thought of using the same fonts anymore, so I tried my hand at designing them. My first designs were cleaned-up scans of found letters or hand-drawn headlines. It was nice because I could tailor the typefaces to the project at hand. As my curiosity grew, I started researching and slowly making real typefaces from the ground up, actually drawing them instead of tuning up scans of my drawings. Looking back, the work was incredibly amateur, but it was a start.

Have you ever thought about setting up shop in another city or country?
Yes, and I think we will eventually move from Minnesota, if only for the sake of experiencing somewhere new, to live in a new city. Currently the foundry is my wife Nicole Dotin and myself [they recently moved to St. Paul, MN]. We're a very small operation and we both have other jobs teaching and designing. We love Minneapolis. We have great family and friends here, so we have several reasons to stay. I've never been impressed with the idea that design needs to happen in large cities to seem connected or vital—I think it can happen anywhere. Especially type design, as it's not dependent on the geographic proximity of customers to your studio. The connection to the wilderness is important to me as well. Type design can be tedious, so time off in the woods is usually when I come up with most of my ideas. We're not in a rush, but eventually, we'll move.

Can you describe the essence of American typography as compared to other Western or European countries? Is there an American typographic zeitgeist or do you think globalism has robbed us of the idea of "local essence"?
It depends on how you look at it. For instance, as a result of smart marketing by some type foundries, American graphic design magazines regularly show the work of House Industries, Adobe, *Emigre*, The Font Bureau and the Hoefler Type Foundry. All are great foundries whose work covers many areas of need—from display work, to rigorous text fonts and special

application situations. Designers are very familiar with most of this work. All of these type foundries, save for Adobe, started as small independents offering something slightly different than the large type houses. So the independent entrepreneurial spirit of the smaller American type houses could be said to be integral to that American essence. By the same token, there is a large body of American work that happens just out of sight. Some of it is very good, and some of it will even rise to the surface, but most of it will forever be stored on hard drives never to be seen by the public. Maybe that's just how it goes.

As far as a style or approach to type design, you could say the work of American typographers is built around revivals, and the work of the Europeans is built around the influence of the broad nib pen. But this isn't the whole picture. What about people like Cyrus Hysmith or Peter Biľak? They don't fit either of the stereotypes assigned to their countries.

How does your studio function day-to-day? You're a two-person operation. Do you plan on staying small?
The day-to-day activities of the studio are very low-key. I do all of the type design, marketing, and Web design, and Nicole handles the database and e-commerce. The revenue generated by the studio is very minor. In turn, I have a few part-time jobs teaching and designing to keep things moving. We are a very young studio, though. I would like to stay small; I'm not sure the foundry would benefit from becoming bigger. And I'm not sure that it could really support a larger structure. Very few type foundries are actually large operations — there are only a handful.

I started Process Foundry because I wanted to make typefaces that I couldn't get, and I'd like to keep it that way. When I was at the Walker, I found myself using a lot of typefaces that were 50 or 60 years old, and it struck me as really strange that these typefaces were picked for contemporary work. In turn, I've tried to make typefaces that would not only fit my current projects, but would also be relevant to other designers' situations. These are goals best suited for the focus of a smaller operation.

What kind of issues do small foundries have to tackle practically and technically?
I think I ran into every single problem possible when I started Process. *laughs* That was mainly because I didn't have any sort of plan to follow. When I first set up the foundry, my only goal was to have a place where people could buy my work. Anything beyond that wasn't considered. E-commerce, marketing, long term planning, and basic survival didn't cross my mind! In retrospect I was just excited to have my work made available to the public.

Of course these things take time if you want to do them well. It's not something that happens in a week or a few months. For instance, every typeface I design has to be hand-spaced, hand-kerned and hand-hinted. A lot of time goes into that work. Ultimately, type designers have to derive pleasure from this process. It's a painful road if they don't.

How long does it take to design a typeface?
It depends on the typeface. I know it's frustrating when type designers say that! For instance, I'm currently finishing up a family of sans serif typefaces that started as a concept in 1999. The work is only being finished now! The actual labor can take as little time as a few weeks of 10-hour days. Extending a type family is another issue. For me, the concept development and direction remains the hardest part. Once that is in place, the production is fairly straightforward.

My process is usually pretty simple. I start out with an idea, which may involve a use-specific typeface, or one for a specific project — or something more complex, like a typeface for a certain size constraint. From that point, I make some small moves on the computer and get some base letters working. Then I let it rest. The computer allows for variations of forms that can be drawn so quickly, and the results are very immediate. It's possible to draw decent forms in a few hours. To avoid disaster, you have to build in time for reflection.

My typefaces all arise from a specific need. After the concept or use is established, I build up a few forms, usually key characters. Then I'll make some working strings of text to get a nice feel for the face. From there I put the project on hold. It's frustrating in a way, because I get enthused, and I want it to go. In graphic design, when you get something started you can take off with it. I used to do that with type design. But when I would come back to the print-outs they were usually terrible! So I started to slow down and give myself some extra time off during the design process.

You mean that you have to force reflection into the design process?
Yes, I usually design the key characters and then I put them away and let them rest. I make prints to look at, but I rarely tinker with them. . After a few weeks, I'll slowly start making changes. To keep things moving, I'm always working on two typefaces. That way I can shift between projects and keep up my enthusiasm.

Type design can be very arduous, but I love the repetition. I was made for it in a way. There's nothing more I like doing than doing things over and over again. But I can't do it all the time. I like to switch back to the other face I'm working on at the time, to keep things fresh.

Then I make prints. I put them on the wall, I carry them in my bag with me, I pull them out at my job or something. It's really a slow burn. I don't push it, but once I get things to a point where I'm happy, the development process is really systematized. I have a series of steps that I follow. Then I give the typeface to my friends so they can test the files. It's ideal to see the typeface used in a printed project before it is made available to the public.

Research and development, right?
Yeah, absolutely. I mean it's really the resources I have at hand.

Do you have a maxim for type design?
I don't have a maxim. But my goal is to make humble, useful, utilitarian typefaces. Ultimately, I hope they're typefaces that designers will find a place for in their work.

So, how do you judge a good typeface?
Judging a typeface is a really strange area. It's always interesting when I show my work to other people, especially non-graphic designers, or art directors. The conversation seems to focus on a specific letter, say, "I really like the 'Q', or I really like this 'R'".

But that's not how a typeface works. A typeface is a collection of all these pieces working together. Alone, they're meaningless, unless the goal is to make a logo or a mark. Strings of letters don't tell the whole story, either.

A font can be judged on how it's used...
How it's used has a lot to do with it. Much of this depends on the user of the typeface, too. For instance, I would argue that Martin Majoor's *Scala* is very well made. It's a smart typeface — it's very fresh, yet it has distinct historical roots, in the camp of Eric Gill. But *Scala* seems to get butchered all the time! Fake italics! Extreme letter spacing! In other cases, I've seen it used in very elegant ways. All of these conditions, not to mention personal taste, make type evaluation a slippery road. Of course this is why we have thousands of typefaces now.

What is your most popular typeface, and how would you explain its success?
My most popular font is *Bryant*, which was released this past Fall of 2002. I never thought

it would be very a very popular typeface. It was something that I created for a specific project, and initially I designed it in only one weight. It was inspired by the stenciling kits that architecture students and shop owners used to use. Its geometric construction lent a neutral feel that I needed for a project that was mainly photographic. The type design needed to act as support for the photographs. I really prefer 'straight ahead' typefaces.

DOCUMENT

Regional notes and corrections

transliterate

It's usually best to start with a capital letter

PRECEDING

Type specimens from *Bryant Light, Regular* and *Bold* (*www. processtypefoundry.com*).

Bryant looked nice on the _Here by Design II_ poster Kindra Murphy designed for the show at the Goldstein Gallery in St. Paul. Do you think she did justice to your font?

Absolutely. She's one of my favorite designers. I'm more influenced by people I know than the people I read about. She's one of the few designers I know who can manage to be informal and smart all in the same project.

Do you see uses of your fonts that you totally disapprove of?

Sure. In many cases, my customers are publishing houses or museums. Most of the designers buying the fonts seem pretty on top of things, so there haven't been too many blunders. On the other hand, there are always instances that make me cringe. *laughs* My current favorite is letterspaced fake italics.

I'm not complaining though. It's naive to assume there should be a higher typographic order governing things. I'm very pleased whenever my work is used. I'm a young designer, so I'm just starting to see my work in use. For the most part, it's been within a context I'm pretty happy with.

Those are good odds...

Maybe, but I think it's really interesting how things work their way through. For instance, for decades now, *Helvetica* has been used in nearly everything.

It's experiencing a revival...

It always is! It's fascinating to watch the path certain fonts take as they descend into ubiquity and banality. It's now common to see, for example, Tobias Frere-Jones' *Interstate* (1993) picked for situations that were once reserved only for *Arial* and *Helvetica*. It's filtered through the cycle of distribution, usage, reuse and discarding, only to be resuscitated for another go at life. Ten years ago, *Interstate* was unknown. For better or worse, it's the American *Helvetica*.

Can a typeface convey the special character of a city? Do you think that is possible?

In the purely aesthetic sense, I'm not sure it can. The typeface might end up being nostalgic and tired. Ultimately, it should be conceptually derived or serve as support for the graphic design of the project. The Twin Cities don't make the A-list with big cities like New York, San Francisco, Chicago and Boston, but we're still very much a large and diverse urban area. The typeface needs to mirror this in some way.

My approach to the Twin Cities typeface was to use the construction of the cities as a metaphor. In a nutshell, the Twin Cities started as a group of small river cities. As need increased and the population grew, the cities expanded outward. My idea was to build a very utilitarian face that served as the hard working version of these river cities. Then, to mirror the expansion of the cities, I included a display version that was filled with idiosyncrasies and details. In retrospect, I

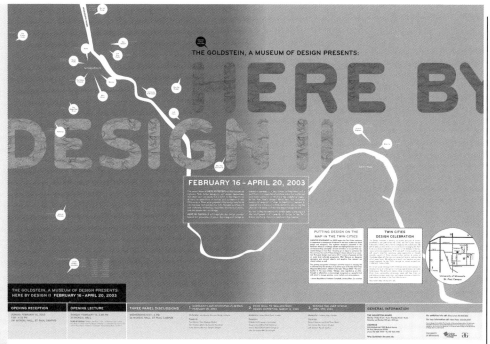

Poster for *Here By Design II*, an exhibition at the University of Minnesota. Olson drew a custom version, *Bryant Super Bold*, for the titling typeface on the front side of the poster.

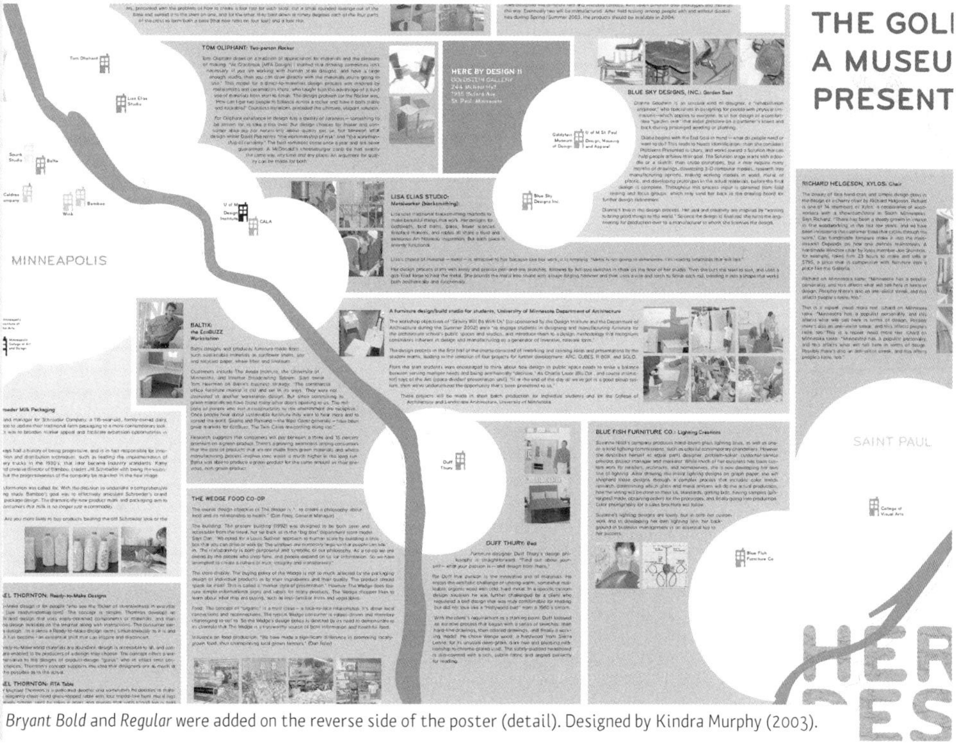

Bryant Bold and *Regular* were added on the reverse side of the poster (detail). Designed by Kindra Murphy (2003).

don't think the faces are dramatic enough to really mirror the expansion of a city.

On the other hand, if there were a project that introduced the font to the public, I think people would understand it. People who live here, especially, could pick up on such nuances.
I think that if a typeface is to represent a city, it's going to have to be more along those lines. Ultimately something that is the result of some very defined conceptual parameters. It could be very nice.

What were some of the other ideas you explored when designing your Twin Cities typeface, and were these ideas in the back of your mind, or did they come out of the brief?
Both. I mentioned the sans serif I'm now completing that was started as a concept back in the late Nineties. This is the typeface that served as the foundation (or river city) for the project.

When I was at the Walker, my thought was to create a sans serif that wasn't out of the blue, but something that was a progression from the old faces that I was using, specifically *Helvetica* and *Akzidenz Grotesk*. A simple idea, but I couldn't get it right. I kept coming up with versions that I'd use for a while, see printed, and then put them aside. This happened several times until finally, in the Spring of 2002, I shelved the project altogether. I told myself it just wasn't meant to be. Then I got the "Typeface: Twin Cities" description in the mail from you in July, and all of a sudden it was the missing piece. The idea for a simple sans face was given the extra direction it needed.

It had found its context?
Absolutely, and I think that had been the problem. It didn't have an application. It was just me without any parameters, dreaming up whatever I wanted—which sometimes can be fun, but I think a typeface is best when it's created for a particular situation.

Many of the forms were sketched out already, but I decided to completely redraw them. They had been redrawn so many times! So I redrew it as a bold weight. And from there, I addressed the project brief, which is where the display version of the typeface comes from. The display version is entirely a reaction to the project.

How do you begin a new typeface design?
All of my typefaces so far have been created for either a specific project or to answer a need that was previously unfulfilled. I think that's common for many type designers. I'm not terribly interested in elaborate or fussy typefaces. I'm more intrigued by the idea that I'm making utilitarian software.

That's an interesting way to put it...
In many ways, type design is really just engineering. Like a puzzle; I'm trying to make all of these pieces work together. I don't usually think of typefaces as elaborate and decorative, so my work tends to be more utilitarian and in some cases, pretty straight ahead. It makes sense though. Most of my graphic design is in support of photographs.

I must say, an afternoon at Home Depot would be more interesting to me than an afternoon at an antiquarian bookstore. I wouldn't turn down the antiquarian bookstore—it would be great. I believe the ideas behind very simple objects like nails and braces are very inspiring. Ordinary objects are so overlooked. I think they still hold some really interesting potential.

What are you working on now?
I'm currently working on finishing up the typefaces that I originally created for the Design Institute's "Typeface: Twin Cities" project [now released as *Locator Display*], and on some new typefaces that are only in the very early conceptual stages. Every time I open them up on the computer, I've forgotten what I've done, and it's like coming back to something new.

HUMBOLDT

YOUR NEIGHBOR AGAIN? OF COURSE. HE LIVES UPSTAIRS.

SNELLING

MAYBE HE CAN'T TAKE HIS SHOES OFF. I THOUGHT OF THAT.

MINNEHAHA

LIKE PERMANENT SHOES? YES! BUT WITH CEMENT SOLES.

LINCOLN

YOU MEAN CONCRETE RIGHT? WHATEVER. HIS FLOORS?

CONCORDIA

GOOD POINT. YOU THINK HE WOULD WEAR THROUGH THEM.

FREMONT

PROCESS TYPE FOUNDRY

Type specimen of Olson's recently released typeface *Locator* and *Locator Display*.

One of our hopes for the "Typeface: Twin Cities" project is that it might entice the public to appreciate typography, or at least, to begin to notice it. Do you think everyone should care about typography?
Typography has a direct effect on the efficiency in our lives, through signage, and information forms, things like that. Of course one great example would be what happened in Florida in the 2000 Presidential Election—that's an example that has been pointed out frequently in the design press. It has been an easy thing to grab on to. However, there are other much more complex and immediate issues than ballot forms. What about type design for the computer or television screen? People rely on screens for information, and in reality, most type designers have given them very little attention, mainly because designing type for the screen is really labor-intensive. It's not like creating typefaces for print. Should people care about it? Sure! But should they be thinking about it all the time? Hell no! If they are, they're either really bored or what they're reading is really illegible.

How do you see the type design profession changing in the future? For example, you just brought up this issue of screen typography. Are there other technologies that will affect typography?
Type design will continue to be exciting. Anyone can have a crack at this. As a result every few years we get some very pure work. As far as technology is concerned, maybe OpenType will change our approach as well. Maybe not. After all, this is still the alphabet. The technologies may have changed but the basic limitations and requirements haven't.

PETER BIL'AK

PETER BIL'AK, GRAPHIC DESIGN & TYPOGRAPHY

THE HAGUE, THE NETHERLANDS

Interviewed in The Hague by Deborah Littlejohn
February 6, 2003

"...a typeface is only a brick—and how you use it is probably more important than the typeface itself."

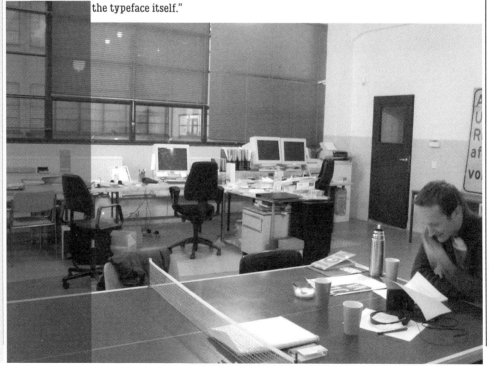

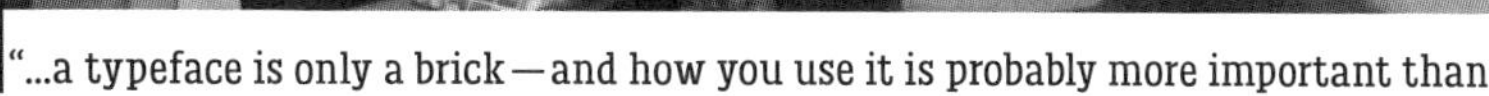

Proposal 1

Reactive typeface

This proposal rejects the idea of a fixed, stamp-like logo, in favor of a dynamically-generated one. Recognition is then achieved not through mere repetition of the same but through variation of forms within a clearly defined frame. Instead of providing fixed sets of letters, the proposed typeface reacts to the physical space, which is available for typesetting. Piece of code within the font determines which alternative characters are used to fit exactly into the text block, which is user-defined. If the user chooses a narrow text block, the font offers narrow alternatives of the characters; if there is more room, they are automatically replaced by its wider alternatives. Every time a logo or string of words is typeset, it might look different according to the size and space available for typesetting.

How does it work?

This font takes advantage of some of the OpenType smart features, namely the JSTF table, which is designed to work with justification of Arabic fonts. By using it with a Latin script, the font takes control over glyph substitution and positioning in justified text. The font itself has options to expand or shrink word and glyph spacing so that text fills the specified line length.

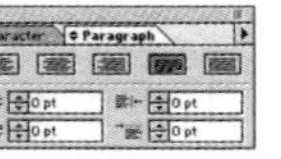

Typeface

Because of its ability to adapt to the space in which it is used, this typeface is ideal to deal with headlines of variable length. Instead of resorting to the abominable practice of stretching type, or inserting double space, the typeface always suggests one of the three different widths to perfectly accommodate copy of just about any length. The proposed version is an elemental cap-only version intended for headline use. A set of lower-case characters is designed for use in text. For hierarchical typesetting, there is a possibility of designing heavier weights of the typeface. The typeface is a sans serif, light, nearly mono-linear typeface generally classified as a Grotesque, or Gothic.

SSS
222
TTT
EEE
DDD
NNN
OOO
WWW

'In what way does your design reflect the Twin Cities?'

The Twin Cities' stable economy, relative prosperity, low unemployment rate, above average per capita earnings and advanced education, give a solid ground for innovations and creativity. The typeface uses intelligent technology in a creative way while continuing in the best traditions of typography and offering a very practical typographic solution.

Various examples of the typeface set in an application that supports OpenType (e.g. Illustrator, InDesign).

Note that the typeface is always in the same point size, yet the shapes of the letters change according to the text block (in light grey) in which it is used.

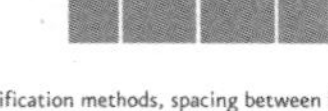

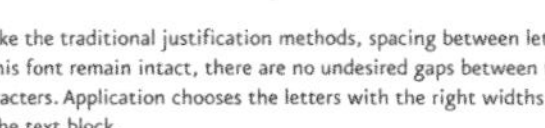

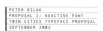

Unlike the traditional justification methods, spacing between letters in this font remain intact, there are no undesired gaps between the characters. Application chooses the letters with the right widths to fit the text block.

PETER BILAK
PROPOSAL 1: REACTIVE FONT
TWIN CITIES TYPEFACE PROPOSAL
SEPTEMBER 2002

Peter Bilák: TCDC typeface proposal 1, board 1.

TWIN CITIES DESIGN 2003

TWIN CITIES DESIGN 2003

TWIN CITIES DESIGN 2003

PETER BILAK
PROPOSAL 1: REACTIVE FONT
TWIN CITIES TYPEFACE PROPOSAL
SEPTEMBER 2002

Peter Bilák: TCDC typeface proposal 1, board 2.

Propoal 2

Awareness of Typography

My second proposal reacts directly to your original brief, and to the objective: 'to raise people's awareness of typography and design in the city'. It is difficult to convey this point through a single typeface, as the general public often has difficulties understanding the difference between the alphabet and the shapes of the letters — typeface. Those two are often confounded; people understand typefaces not as something 'designed', but as something that simply 'exists'.

Natural reaction would not be to present a new font but a variety of them, proved by time, each designed for different historical and practical reasons. A font that is not exclusive but inclusive; a font that compresses the history of type design and typography into one story.

History of Typography

I propose to celebrate design in the Twin Cities in 2003 by choosing different fonts for each day of the year. 356 different fonts for 356 days. The fonts are ordered chronologically, starting with Gutenberg's invention in 1453 and concluding with the latest typeface of 2003. 550 years of the development of typography are divided into 356 days. Every time something needs to be printed, a respective font is used. Underneath the message (poster, advertising, press release, etc.) is a small reference crediting the typeface and type designer. A collection of printed material about TCDC becomes a collection of type specimens used in context, documenting evolution of type design.

How does it work?

The user simply works with one font, as it would have been a fixed static font, and small custom application does the work. When the user selects the typeface 'History' from the font menu, the computer looks at the current date, and retrieves the font from the database that is attributed for that day. This project presupposes collaboration with a large type foundry (Adobe, Bitstream, FontShop, etc) which lends its library of fonts to promote each of them for a day.

'In what way does your design reflect the Twin Cities?'

Although I have been to The Twin cities only once, I have noticed the efforts to promote art and design in the city, and many places where one can experience the cutting edge in the visual arts. This proposed solution is an opportunity to pay similar attention to typography.

Conclusion

This proposal is not about formal or aesthetical solutions. It is not about choosing the best typeface, but about gaining a sense of typography. In this proposal, meaning is derived less from individual elements than from the relationships between them.

01/2003 02/2003 03/2003 04/2003 05/2003 06/2003 07/2003 08/2003 09/2003 10/2003 11/2003 12/2003

Twin Cities Design 2003

Twin Cities Design 2003

Twin Cities Design 2003

Twin Cities Design 2003

Twin Cities Design 2003

Twin Cities Design 2003

Twin Cities Design 2003

Twin Cities Design 2003

sample

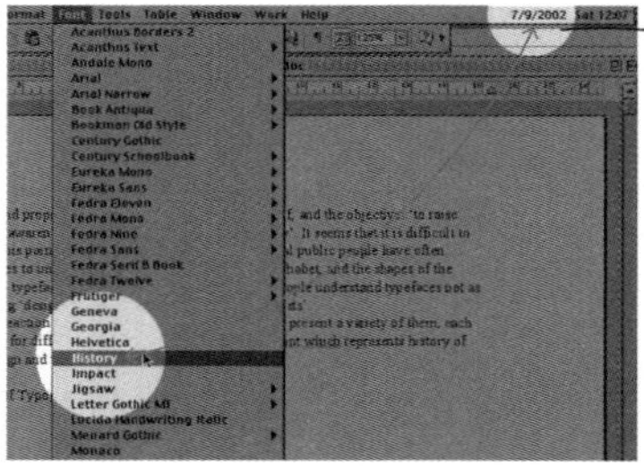

Sample selection of fonts. To cover all the days, a proper historical reserach would have to be conducted.
(There is also a possibility to to change fonts weekly, and to choose 52 fonts.)

1453 Gutenberg's Bible
1470 Jenson
1490 Bembo
1499 Aldus Manutius
1530 Garamond, Claude Garamond
1734 Caslon, William Caslon
1757 Baskerville, John Baskerville
1764 Pierre Simon Fournier le Jeune
1785 Didot, François Ambroise Didot
1788 Bell, John Bell
1790 Bodoni, Giambattista Bodoni
1898 Akzindent Grotesque
1900 Century, M.F.Benton
1908 News Gothic, M.F.Benton
1915 London Underground, Edward Johnson
1917 Cochin, Sol Hess
1923 Neuland, Rudolph Koch
1926 universal-bauer
1928 Futura, Paul Renner
1929 Gaudy Sans, FW. Gaudy
1930 city type, Georg trump
1930 Metro, W.A. Dwinggins
1931 Gill, Eric Gill
1932 Times New Roman, Stanley Morison
1938 Bell Gothic, Chauncey Griffith
1950 Janco, Marcel Janco
1951 Berling, K.E. Forsberg
1953 Mistral, Roger Excoffon
1954 Univers, Adrian Frutiger
1955 Choc, Roger Excoffon
1957 Miedinger, Helvetica
1958 Calypso, Roger Excoffon
1962 Antique Olive, Roger Excoffon
1964 Sabon, Tschichold
1966 Serifa, Adrian Frutiger
1967 New alphabet, Wim Crouwel
1970 Avant Garde Gothic, Lubalin
1975 Bookman, Ed Benguiat
1978 Bell Centenial, Mathew Carter
1979 Benguiat Gothic
1982 Cosmos, Gustav Jaeger
1983 Barmeno, Hans Reichel
1984 Meta, Erik Spiekermann
1986 Centennial, Adrian Frutiger
1987 Amerigo, Gerard Unger
1988 Avenir, Adrian Frutiger
1989 Arial, Robin Nicholas
1990 Corporate, Kurt Weidemann
1991 Scala, Martin Majoor
1992 Myriad, Robert Slimbach
2000 Profile, Martin Wenzel
2001 Fedra Sans, Peter Bilak
2002 Sauna, Underware

text -> date -> database -> font

Twin Cities Design

Serifa, Adrian Frutiger, 1966

PETER BILAK
PROPOSAL 2: HISTORY
TWIN CITIES TYPEFACE PROPOSAL
SEPTEMBER 2002

Peter Bilák: TCDC typeface proposal 2, board 1.

Twin Cities Design 2003
Garamond, by Claude Garamond 1530

Twin Cities Design 2003
Akzindenz Grotesk, Bertold Foundry, 1896

Twin Cities Design 2003
Times, Stanley Morison, 1932

Twin Cities Design 2003
Verdana, Matthew Carter, 1996

Twin Cities Design 2003
Fedra Sans, Peter Bilak, 2001

PETER BILAK
PROPOSAL 2: HISTORY
TWIN CITIES TYPEFACE PROPOSAL
SEPTEMBER 2002

Peter Bilák: TCDC typeface proposal 2, board 2.

DEBORAH LITTLEJOHN: Where are you from?
PETER BIĽAK: I'm from Slovakia. I was born in Czechoslovakia, but it no longer exists. When I returned from my studies abroad, it was a different country: divorced, renamed and changed.

You attended the Academy of Fine Arts in Bratislava, studied in England, the U.S., the Atelier National de Création Typographique in Paris, and at the Jan van Eyck Akademie in Maastricht. And now you have set up your studio here in The Hague. Do you consider yourself a Dutch or a Slovak designer? Or are these distinctions not so important?
Obviously I am not a Dutch designer, but I am influenced by plenty of different things here that have changed my thinking about design. Living and working in a foreign country speeds up the process of personal development. I observe local influences, and at the same time, I become immune to them in some way.

National distinctions are necessary descriptions, but describing people solely by their place of birth is reductive, and I try to avoid that. It doesn't say too much about the personality of the individual, and it becomes less important for me. One thing is clear, though: being born in Czechoslovakia, studying in different countries, and living here in Holland have had tremendous influence on my work.

Is the vibe from any one of these cities where you have worked more important to you?
I am influenced by my prolonged stay in the Netherlands, but I am influenced by everything that surrounds me: food I eat, music I listen to, books I read. People I meet along the way become the primary source of influence — they lead to future projects and collaborations.

You are teaching in the post-graduate course at the Royal Academy for Fine & Applied Arts in The Hague.
Yes, I teach in the department where Erik van Blokland and Just van Rossum teach. I had heard of the school and knew about some of the graduates, like Erik and Just, long before I moved to the Netherlands, and to find myself teaching here is a strange coincidence. I am probably the only teacher at the Academy who hasn't studied here as well. The school has a solid reputation and traditions, so I have had to think a lot about what else I can bring. I leave the practicalities of type design up to other teachers here who do it very well, and I try to concentrate on broader issues, for example, the influence of language on type and its appearance — or how the Latin alphabet relates to other writing systems. These questions also reappear in my work and teaching is an opportunity for a discussion.

Does teaching prevent you from becoming set in a "type designer" niche?
It is a natural part of my work; regular studio work is complemented by academic discussion, the exchange of ideas, and the exploration of themes that interest me. Making a magazine (*Dot Dot Dot*, with Stuart Bailey) is a bit of the same. We are making it to develop certain themes that are outside of our own work.

Stuart Bailey and Peter Biľak, *Dot Dot Dot*, issues 1–5, 2000–0

Have you ever considered changing the home base of your studio to another city or another country?
I don't think it was a decision to move here to begin with. I followed a path that led me here. This path started a long time ago, and I am not

sure where else it will lead. I ended up here because of a series of events that happened after I left Paris, and was staying in Bratislava. Perhaps it was an idea in the back of my mind, but also there were events beyond my control which helped make it happen. I moved to Holland shortly after my apartment in Bratislava burned down. Other events led me from Maastricht to The Hague. I enjoy being here now very much. I don't have plans to move elsewhere right now, but again, that could easily change.

Your studio is as multidisciplinary as you are multinational — there is the writing, the editing of *Dot Dot Dot*, and you design typefaces, as well as books. Do you consider yourself an editor, a typographer, a writer, or a book designer?
It makes it easier to present yourself if you can describe yourself by the work you are doing and the media you specialize in. But I prefer to not define myself; I really enjoy the diversity — and I think the fact that I design books, typefaces, websites and video, as well as the editing and writing, makes each of these activities stronger. As a creator of fonts, it is easier to use them; as a writer, it is easier for me to edit and work with text; and experience with web design influences the print design as well.

On the other hand it also makes it more difficult. Being a designer of new fonts makes me want to choose the old ones; writing text makes me not want to design other people's texts. But returning to your previous questions, no, I don't have a business card that spells out what I do...

You have a nice set-up at this studio...
We all do something different — Paul is a pure and dedicated type designer. Taco is a web developer. Edwin and Bart are programmers, and Renate does print design. We often end up working together, and at the same time, enjoy the fact that each is completely independent.

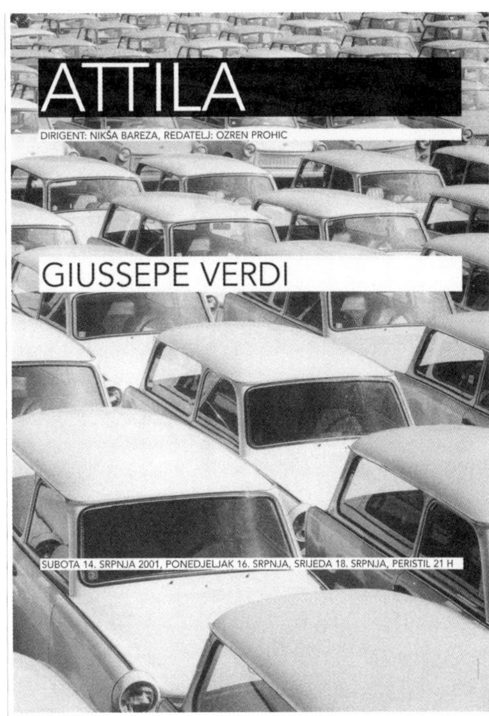

Biľak's poster for the Giussepe Verdi's *Attila*, Split Summer Theatre Festival, 2001

How do you judge a good typeface?
I don't think there are clear rules for judging the qualities of a typeface — it's more about how the typeface relates to the time in which it is made, or how it relates to the particular situation in which it is used. That's why it would be tricky to ask "how would you judge a typical baroque typeface now?" and "how would you have judged it 300 years ago?" The typeface hasn't changed — the way of *looking at it* has changed. That's why you may not appreciate something as much now as when it was done years ago. So I don't think it is something inherent in the font or the typeface — a parallel might be in other forms of art, like painting or literature. It's not really the amount or the quality of the words that you use in literature, but more a question of whether the words are relevant today.

It might be helpful to get beyond the discrimination of values — every typeface exhibits some sort of beauty, and it really depends on the context in which it is used. In order to escape aesthetic judgments, some type designers present their activity as "problem solving", which is something I don't entirely agree with, because that would mean as soon as the type designer solves all the problems, there is no longer a reason to design typefaces. And I think there must be some other motivation to draw typefaces, that could also influence how to look at typefaces — something that is motivated by the creation itself.

Again I'll have to make parallels with other forms of art — I think it was Herman Broch, an Austrian writer who said, "The sole reason for a novel is to discover what only a novel can discover." I can't exactly apply that to type design, but it does help me look at it as something other than "problem solving." There must be something that drives a new typeface to be made. It's in the way history itself has always been the inspiration for making fonts. It is an applied accumulation of knowledge — an internal logic of the activity itself — where type designers react to the previously made fonts. So looking at one artifact, you see the previous attempts and failures. And that's what makes it easier to think about it in a larger context, and easier to judge and discuss it.

Should the general public care about type design?

I don't think they have to. It is such a very specialized profession. I don't read highly specialized trade publications such as *Plumbing Today*. Then again, even if I'm not so interested in plumbing, I use it every day, and I'm happy that it's there, and that someone else thinks about it and makes it work well.

Perhaps people only care about design when it doesn't work properly or when it hurts, or — God forbid — if it kills them. But it is in those moments when one is forced to realize that it is important.

That's right. You see it often in the redesign of the newspaper; people notice some change, which they cannot even describe, and usually they dislike it. *laughs* The problem of presenting the relevance of type design takes place at a level of discussion that can be very technical and tiresome — and that's a disturbing aspect of it, which isolates it from other disciplines.

What is your most popular typeface and how would you explain its success?

In terms of sales, I know exactly — I have the records. But that doesn't say anything about the font itself. I designed this font, *Eureka* — it is quite a complex family. In terms of sales, it is my most successful font. *Eureka* is also the reason that I designed this new font, *Fedra Sans* and *Fedra Serif*. I'm saying it's the reason, because having made *Eureka*, there were many unresolved issues and problems I tackled while not having much experience at the time. There are plenty of mistakes and imperfections in *Eureka*, and *Fedra* was my attempt to fix them, without actually modifying an existing font.

Did those imperfections only come to light when you sent *Eureka* out into the world, and people started using it, and you thought, "oh gosh, it's not supposed to do that..."

Exactly. I was so focused on certain details of the font that I forgot about other things. When I saw *Eureka* used for the first time in Dutch, I was shocked. The long words and plenitude of 'g's made it look very awkward. But the font was published by then, and it was difficult to change things. Some things also became features of the font, so it didn't make sense to change them. When I started *Fedra*, I was able to change the whole skeleton and the complete principles of the typeface, because it was a new product. So it's not just about correcting the outlines of the previous font, but more about a different way of looking at the same type design problem. I am much more pleased

FF Eureka Serif

$%&'()*#0123456789.,:;
ABCDEFGHIJKLMNOP
QRSTUVWXYZ[\]?!@{}
abcdefghijklmnopqrst
uvwxyzÄÅÇÉÑÖÜáàâä
ãåçéèêëíìîïñóòôöõúùûü
ctstztnhfifjflffffiffifb
fkfhæœø¢£§&•¶ß©™
~+<=>¬ÆØ¥ªº¿¡ƒ«»ÂÁ
ÀÃÕŒ–—“”‘’ÿŸ‹›†‡·„
ÊËÈÍÎÏÌÓÔÒÚÛÙ½¼…

a g

The original drawings for *FF Eureka* date from 1995. By the end of the year first PostScript versions were ready. Already first version were tested in real situations. In four years of development *Eureka* found it application in books, magazines, brochures, posters, television screen and even post-stamps. Each printed sample returned to the author for reexamination, which resulted in improving and completing the family. The general consensus is that the best fonts had been designed for a particular purpose. Eureka had been designed for the bilingual text of *Transparency* book. The typeface works especially well for languages with accented characters. You may have noticed already that text set in *Garamond* looks the best in the French language, *Bodoni* looks great in Italian, and *Baskerville* in English, however in a different language they all have a different character. Most of the type designers today come from the countries which do not face a problem of accented characters. In English and Dutch are accents very rare. Other countries with linguistic particularities, however, have serious problems with using those typefaces. The x-height as we see often in contemporary western fonts is too large, and a typeface is therefore unable to accommodate adequate punctuation. The resulting accents are too small. However, in many languages the accents are an integral part of the alphabet and shouldn't be reduced in size and importance. To obtain the proper type rhythm in the text proportions of the typeface were adjusted. The height of the ascenders and descenders is 1.7 times the x-height. This relatively small x-height leaves room for longer descenders and ascenders which in turn better accommodate accents and punctuation, whilst giving the typeface a distinctive character. The large serifs visually balance the larger accents. Designed by Peter Bilak.

Fedra Sans

by Peter Biľak

A new sans serif, originally designed as a corporate font for one of those huge companies; now completed, updated, and ready to use in all formats. *Available in five weights, with three different numeral systems, real italics, small capitals, and expert sets full of ligatures, fractions, arrows, symbols and other useful little things.*

Aa *Aa*

← ↖ ↑ ↗ → ↘ ↓ ↙

Fedra Sans *Light*
Fedra Sans *Book*
Fedra Sans *Normal*
Fedra Sans *Medium*
Fedra Sans *Bold*

Đ đ Ł ł Š š Ý ý Þ þ Ž ž ½ ¼ ¹ ¾ ³ ² ¦
- × ! # $ % & ' ( ) * + , - . / 0 1 2
3 4 5 6 7 8 9 : ; = > < ? @ A B C D E
F G H I J K L M N O P Q R S T U V W X
Z Y [\ ] ^ _ ` a b c d e f g h i j k
l m n o p q r s t u v w x y z { | } ~
Ä Å Ç É Ñ Ö Ü á à â ä ã å ç é è ê ë í
ì î ï ñ ó ò ô ö õ ú ù û ü † ° ¢ £ § •
¶ ß ® © ™ ´ ¨ ≠ Æ Ø ∞ ± ≤ ≥ ¥ µ ∂ Σ Π
π ∫ ª º Ω æ ø ¿ ¡ ¬ √ ƒ ≈ ∆ « » … À Ã
Õ Œ Œ œ – — “ ” ‘ ’ ÷ ◊ ÿ Ÿ ⁄ € ‹ › fi
fl ffi ffl ff fk fh fj ‡ · ‚ „ ‰ Â Ê Á Ë È Í Î
Ï Ì Ó Ô g Ò Ú Û Ù ı ˆ ˜ ¯ ˘ ˙ ˚ ¸ ˝ ˛

www.typotheque.com
sales@typotheque.com
Fax +31-84-831 6741

Type specimens of *Eureka Serif* (left) and *Fedra Sans* (right).

with it now, although it's hard to tell if it's going to be more popular.

It seems that there will always be some little imperfection to be found...
Which is fine. The idiosyncrasies and the quirkiness become features, contributing to the personality of the font. And the fact that it sells well confirms it. There are plenty of examples of other fonts that are beautiful because of the imperfections.

What is the most unusual or unexpected context in which you've found your type designs used?
I started publishing and distributing typefaces directly through *www.typotheque.com*, my website, and I now have a very direct relationship with the people who buy my typefaces. I resisted doing this for years because I was afraid I would turn into another font shop, which has the connotation of selling out. It took some time to get more comfortable with the idea of exchanging my energy for money, and now I am glad I did it. I am now able to have this direct contact with people, and see the results of how they use my typefaces—and even give advice on how they can be used. Though this is not to say that I want to control the use of my fonts. It is a discussion.

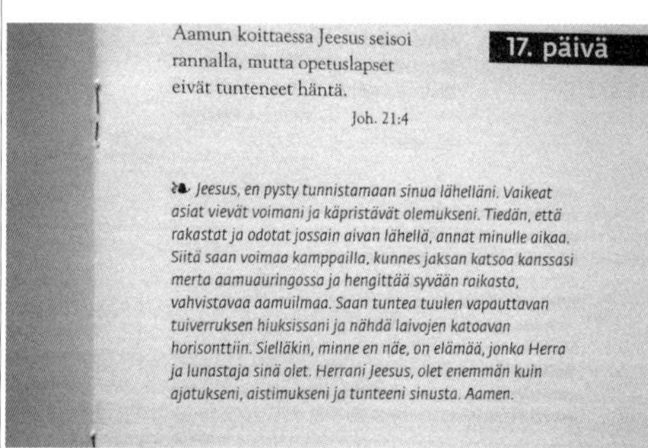

17. päivä

Aamun koittaessa Jeesus seisoi
rannalla, mutta opetuslapset
eivät tunteneet häntä.

Joh. 21:4

Jeesus, en pysty tunnistamaan sinua lähelläni. Vaikeat asiat vievät voimani ja käpristävät olemukseni. Tiedän, että rakastat ja odotat jossain aivan lähellä, annat minulle aikaa. Siitä saan voimaa kamppailla, kunnes jaksan katsoa kanssasi merta aamuauringossa ja hengittää syvään raikasta, vahvistavaa aamuilmaa. Saan tuntea tuulen vapauttavan tuiverruksen hiuksissani ja nähdä laivojen katoavan horisonttiin. Sielläkin, minne en näe, on elämää, jonka Herra ja lunastaja sinä olet. Herrani Jeesus, olet enemmän kuin ajatukseni, aistimukseni ja tunteeni sinusta. Aamen.

Fedra Sans set for a Finnish book of prayers. Designed by Minna Törrönen for Raision seurakunta.

My new typeface, *Fedra Sans*, was recently used for the identity of a gay festival. The very same week, it was used for a new Finnish book of prayers. It is the same font, so it makes me wonder how on earth they both came to the decision to choose it. Although I never considered it would be used like this, I do try to see why. Also, the fact that my fonts are used in different languages and contexts—and by different people—is really exciting for me.

How long does it take to design a typeface?
It depends. When I was doing *Eureka*, it took me a very long time. From the point where I started sketching, to the point where it was public at FontShop, it took five or six years—which doesn't mean that I worked on it for six years, because I took breaks during that time. With the new typeface, *Fedra*, it has taken less time. I made the *Sans* in about six months, which was surprising for me. I am now working on the serif counterpart of the *Fedra Sans* font, which is based on the same skeleton. I have been working on it for more than two years and only now is it getting to be ready for publishing.

Although the design of a typeface can go very fast, there are many things that go into it. For example, having the luxury of time, and not having a deadline, extends the problem. If a typeface is commissioned, I have a clear deadline and am therefore focused on the work. And then, there are some unexpected delays: when *Fedra* was nearly done and I finally had a full version that I could use, we had a burglary here in the studio, and my computers were stolen. I lost all the work including the backup. So I had to go back to the very beginning. Because I had to do it again, it made it very much like a reverse-engineering problem. Because I knew the previous end-result, I had a chance to review the process, and I could do some modifications.

I had a version of *Fedra Serif* I thought was final a year ago. I used it in an IndieFonts book, but now I still have a few months of work to do in order to complete it properly. After seeing some test prints I thought it wasn't working well enough, so I decided to redraw it. So, it's a back and forth process and that's why it's hard to define the time it takes to design a typeface. It takes as long as you want it to take.

Can a typeface communicate the special character of a city?
I don't know. It's probably too ambitious to think that a single typeface can tell what's particular about a city. After all, a typeface is only a brick—and how you use it is probably more important than the typeface itself. So to say that the font itself can make such a difference is a bit exaggerated. At the same time, it's easier to make a difference if you have a good building material. It's probably easier to talk about its uniqueness, and to extend it further and to present the city as a unique place, because of the typeface.

What were some of the challenges you tackled with your Twin Cities typeface proposal which also required OpenType technology? Were these ideas you were already developing or did they come out of the brief?
They came out of the project, out of the brief you sent last summer. The problem was that I had the feeling you might be looking for some clever kind of modular system. And also I wasn't sure how to go about it—whether I should go with my assumptions about your expectations, or should suggest something completely different. And then I started to look at other things, for example, data about what makes the Twin Cities a unique place. And it made it difficult and too forced to translate that into a font.

I started playing with my first idea, which used OpenType, and I wasn't completely convinced it was the right one. And then I got another idea which I thought was better, and related to the part in your brief that said you wanted to make people more aware of typography in the city. We just spoke about it now, about this accumulation of history. I came to the conclusion that you cannot raise people's awareness of typography by designing a new font. It lacks reference; it is isolated. How to present the idea of type design to a public that doesn't know too much about the history of typography? Focusing on a single typeface, however unique and interesting, I thought was a misunderstanding of the brief and would result in the further marginalization of type design. The only way to do it, then, would be to show the origins of type design, to show that it does have a history, and that whatever is made now is in some way a reaction to these failures and successes. And this was the second proposal.

In hindsight, I feel that I should have not sent the first proposal because it contradicts the second one, which I think was stronger—because the system itself is the exploration of these issues. And it addresses this idea of not talking about typography as a problem-solving activity, but as something that is driven by *itself*, by the history of type design. So the idea came from the Design Institute's brief sent last July, and it emphasized the fact that typography has been around for hundreds of years...

I thought it was a good proposal—it was similar to a conceptual art project.
I was pleased with it. But at the same time, I sort of knew it would not be something the Design Institute would want to use...

I think the problem was more in the implementation: how would we communicate this idea? Would we have to put a printed artifact out into the world each and every day for our audience to understand the identity and see the complexity of the project and that idea? That would be impossible...
I am sure there are a number of solutions for this, but that is secondary now. Unlike my first proposal, I felt that the "History" proposal responded very directly to the assignment. One thing that is pretty predictable about my first proposal, and the use of OpenType, is that

it's really a designer's thing to take the latest technology and try to integrate it into their work. I was trying to explore the potential and make something that was very unique for a city. Although it was a solution that could work, I felt it was too much of a presentation of the power of technology, rather than an idea coming from the font. It was too dependent upon the context in which it is presented.

Can you talk about your working process? How does your studio operate day-to-day?
I like to see that the project itself inspires the result—the outcome—and that I don't have a set of predefined answers about the way that I work, that I almost have to "relearn" everything. With type design, it is a bit different because the constraints and limitations are much clearer than in other aspects of work. I am interested in converting the limitations into inspiration.

I wish there were a way to combine this "micro and macro" view of design into one view—the type designer's obsession with detail and the graphic designer's knowledge of the whole. Graphic designers know that everything has its consequences: they understand relationships, that if the paper is changed, that affects the size, the font, the colors—everything. This is something that gets obscured in type design, because there is so much looking at the detail, and the same problems must be solved every time. Type designers go through the same process, which is very repetitive, and is not necessarily something common to other design disciplines. I wish there were a way to merge these two ways of thinking into one.

You collaborate with Stuart on *Dot Dot Dot* and you have several colleagues here in the studio. Is your work primarily collaborative?
With Stuart, it's really just the magazine that we work on together. Here in the studio, it's a bit different. Everyone is loosely collaborating, but not necessarily. Most of the time I am working individually. And I don't have a rhythm, like "on Monday I do type design" and "on Wednesday I do web design." The work is quite comfortable, easygoing, and not too stressful...

How do you see the profession and practice of typography and type design changing in the future?
I don't expect many things to change. It became a "thing" to live in expectation of the future, or, on the other hand, live isolated in the past. If one focuses on the work itself, which reflects the conditions in which we work, the result is necessarily contemporary work. My understanding of the future is continued contemporariness. The means of execution might change, but that is not so important.

CONOR MANGAT
INFLECTION
KENTFIELD, CALIFORNIA

Interviewed in San Francisco by Janet Abrams
February 17, 2003

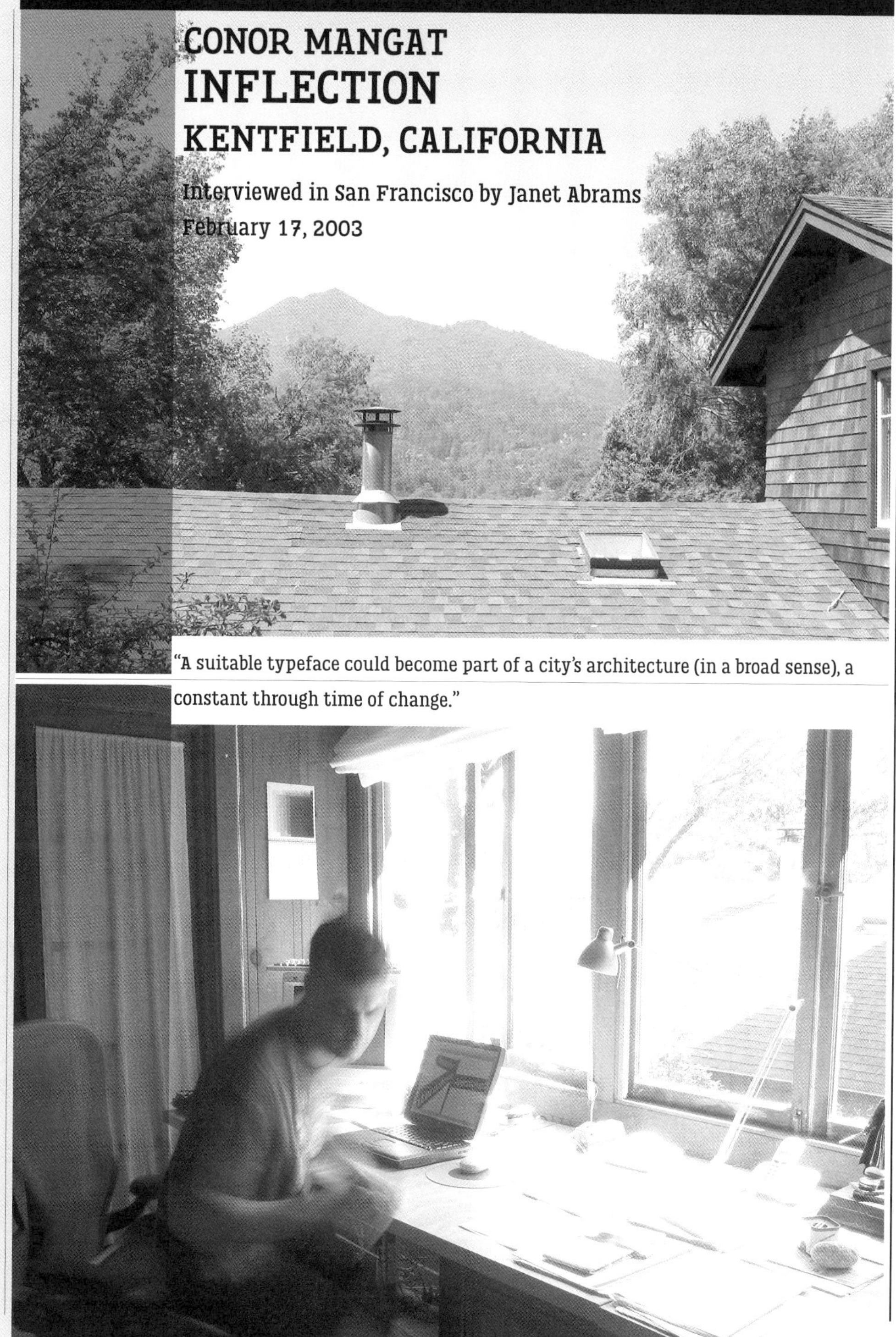

"A suitable typeface could become part of a city's architecture (in a broad sense), a constant through time of change."

TWIN CITIES DESIGN 2003

Twin Cities Design 2003

TWIN CITIES DESIGN 2003

Twin Cities Design 2003

Conor Mangat: TCDC typeface proposal, board 1.

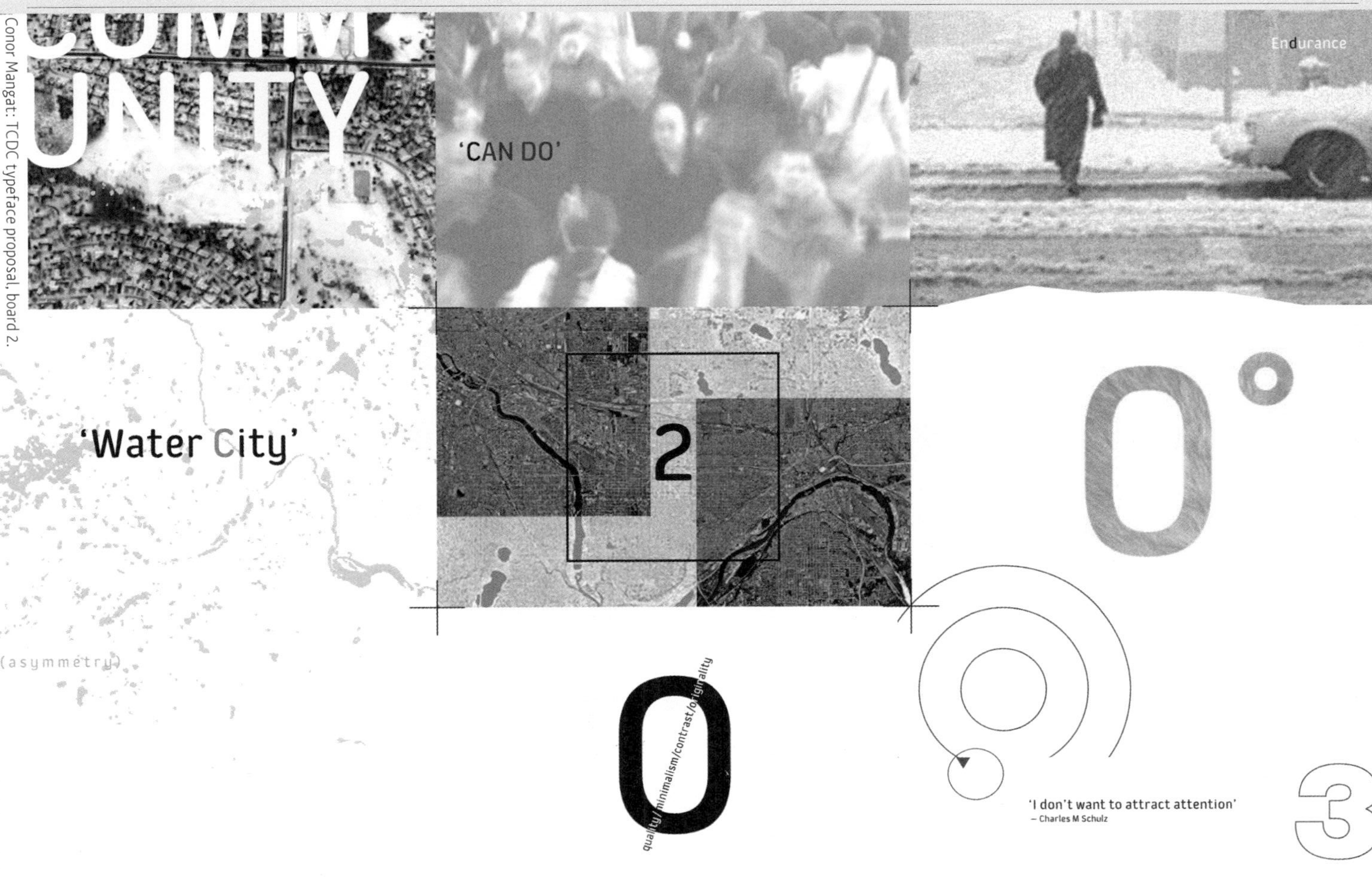

Conor Mangat: TCDC typeface proposal, board 2.

Conor Mangat: TCDC typeface proposal, board 3.

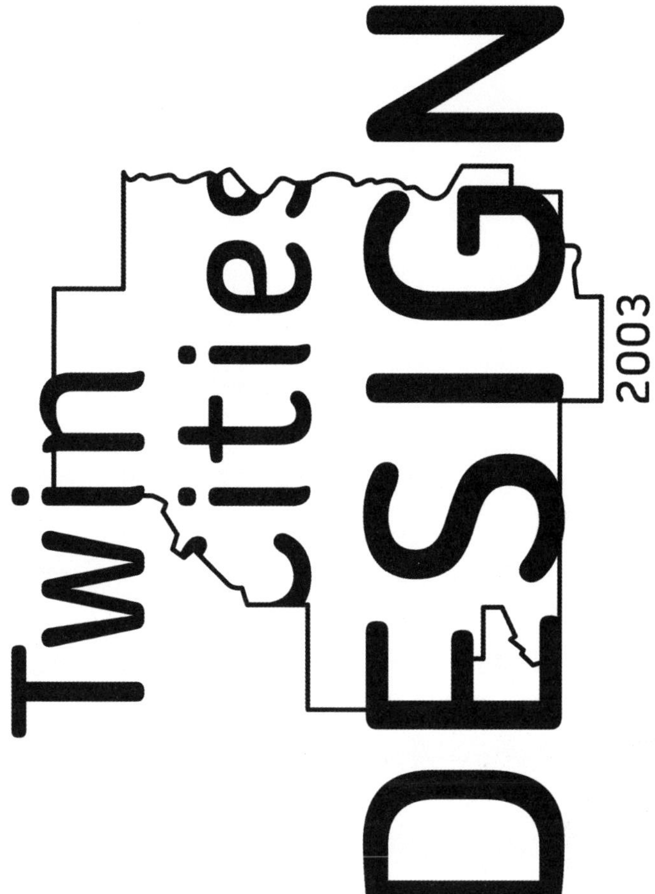

Conor Mangat: TCDC typeface proposal, board 4.

JANET ABRAMS: **Where are you from?**
CONOR MANGAT: South East London, Bromley to be precise.

Where exactly is that?
Suburbia. Twenty minutes by train (on a good day), and you're in the middle of London. Ten minutes in the car the other direction and it's countryside.

Did you grow up there, or did you move from somewhere else?
I grew up there — born and raised.

You're a designer, a typographer — do you consider yourself one or the other?
I've settled on "typographic designer" mainly because "typographer" is fairly specific and doesn't encompass my training as a graphic designer. One of Erik Spiekermann's [founder of MetaDesign, now with offices in San Francisco, Berlin and Zürich] maxims is that the typographer works from the word up and the graphic designer works from the picture down; detail before concept, I guess. And I'm probably happier — more comfortable — working with words and letters than I am with images — which is not to say that I can't do both, but that's mostly where my leanings are.

Let's hear you describe your work path from Bromley to MetaDesign in San Francisco.
I did my undergraduate studies at Ravensbourne College of Design and Communication, which is in Bromley.

It's not a College of Art?
No, it used to be. They got rid of the Fine Art degree programs before I got there, so it was very much design and communication.

What other kind of courses besides Graphic Design did they have?
Fashion, Furniture, Product design. Aside from Graphic Design, there was a separate TV school, which has since been absorbed into the main school. There was a strong emphasis on the broadcast side of things for a while — a big money maker after all — and it has subsequently panned out with a general technological focus: interaction design, new media, motion graphics, and so forth.

When were you there?
Between '88 and '91. I graduated into the depths of recession and spent a year doing very little indeed. Then in Autumn '92 I went to California Institute of the Arts in Valencia, California.

Did you get some kind of fellowship for that?
I got a partial scholarship, yeah.

How brave of you to leap out of England! How did you make that decision to leave home?
I wanted to do postgraduate study, but I didn't really like the available options I had at home. I had an interview at the Royal College of Art in London, but nothing came of that. I always had certain reservations about the Royal College, though.

What were those?
It seems like the focus of the course changes drastically every few years, every time the department head changes. And some of the projects I saw seemed kind of dumb. I wasn't too sure what to make of it all. During an Open House day, when one of the tutors was asked about reasons for studying there, his answer was that "It's all about meeting people". Surely there had to be more to it than just networking.

So how did you find out about CalArts?
Our Head of Department at Ravensbourne, Peter Rea, had taught at various schools in the U.S., such as the Rhode Island School of Design in Providence and Otis Parsons in Los Angeles, so he had all these connections. He came to Ravensbourne the same time that I did, and he instituted an exchange program where students from there came here and vice versa. Actually, I'm jumping ahead, because it

really started with a poster I saw on the wall at college, from (I think) some college in Canada saying "Why don't you come over here and study?" I thought "that's kind of stupid, why would I go over there?" Then I thought "if so many overseas students come over here, what's to stop me from going somewhere else to study?" So that kind of planted the seed.

Was *Emigre* being published already?
Yeah, this was probably '90 or thereabouts, so I was aware of it. Anyway, I let it lie for a while, particularly considering the costs involved, which seemed astronomical compared to education in the UK. Then, during the year of self-unemployment that came after that, I looked into it in more detail.

And you found you could get a scholarship to CalArts?
Well that happened right at the end, because I had gone through all the application stuff, and they said they didn't really grant money to foreign students in their first year. I'd tried to get funding from elsewhere, to no avail, so I wrote a pleading letter and said, "I'd really like to come — could you find some money?" and they did.

Excellent!
So off I went to CalArts. Looking back, it was a huge risk because I didn't visit the college before I decided, and I didn't really research it terribly deeply, as I would now. But now you have the Web, which wasn't available then. And the reason I knew about CalArts was because the school's admissions catalog had been featured in *Blueprint* magazine [the British design magazine] sometime before — their design faculty Lorraine Wild, Ed Fella and Jeff Keedy designed this catalog that had little holes cut out of the cover. I thought it was really clever... *laughs* and it just stuck in my mind. Actually, when I was researching colleges at the Fulbright Commission in London, there was a CalArts poster on the wall, and it reminded me of the hole-y catalog, so I thought I'd look into it further.

So, CalArts was...
'92 – '94. And then, I moved to Chicago for eight months in '94–'95 with a friend because I had no real reason to stay in LA .

What did you do there?
I lived downtown, and I was able to do a bit of freelance work.

Did you like it in Chicago?
It was ok. I didn't mind it — but I didn't really have a job (or a long term visa), so I did what I could — quite a lot of work at the type foundry Monotype and other freelance projects. That was kind of a regrouping period for me anyway, and I was looking at a few other places outside Chicago. Actually, the very last letter that I wrote was to MetaDesign in San Francisco; by that point, I was ready to clear up and go home to London.

How has the culture of San Francisco and MetaDesign changed your design?
It was a good fit, which is part of the reason I am back there now. They still have a very international perspective, given Meta's European origins. But the type of work — culturally, geographically, I don't know if it has made a huge difference...

Los Angeles must have been impactful — you had just left London. Don't tell me you just took to it like a duck to water...
I think it was just being away from home — whether or not it was Los Angeles — because basically I spent my undergraduate years at home living with the parents. So it was really just that period of growing up. Whether or not it would have been drastically different had I been in Amsterdam or Nottingham, or wherever, I don't know. Probably.

I think you're underplaying it, Conor! What about the landscape?
How so?

Didn't that have any impact on your work, I mean Hollywood? Big desert? Palm trees?
I don't think so necessarily. I suppose there's a certain freedom or looseness compared to England, perhaps, a general attitude...

What about San Francisco?
Less so here. It's more conservative; less whacked out! Rudy VanderLans says coming to the States from Holland had a huge effect on him, and that's where the idea of *Emigre* magazine came from. He said it was all about the freedom to do whatever you wanted. Which is a perfectly valid argument, but I don't necessarily feel that strongly about it.

Can you say what being in America has done to your philosophy and type design and aesthetic? What have you been able to do here that might have been different in London?
I think maybe it comes down to practical issues of working, like when I went back to London, people weren't interested in any kind of flexible relationship. There seemed to be this rather Victorian attitude that unless you're at your desk 40 hours a week, you're useless—or not to be trusted. Whereas the last couple of years here in the U.S., I was able to telecommute from home almost all the time.

Who were you working for, telecommuting?
Metro Newspapers, a Silicon Valley publisher. I'd go to the office now and again, get the work done, and nobody complained—it was fine. Whereas, when I went back to England, I was trying to study and teach a bit, and do a bit of this and a bit of that...

But now you've gone back to MetaDesign a second time. What's your title there now?
Design Director.

And what does that mean?
I direct design. *[laughs]*

But how encompassing is it? Are there lots of design directors?
No, there's only me.

How big is the company here?
Twelve people.

That's down?
Yeah, it was about 60-ish a couple of years ago. When I joined the first time I was the 12th; when I left in '97 it was pushing 30, and then it followed a typical dot.com trajectory and ballooned up to about 60. Now it's back down to 12.

And what did you do at Reading University? You did a thesis as well?
We're getting ahead... My time at CalArts was basically for two years; you go through all the immigration paper work, you have two years and then you have to leave. But then when I got here, the story was, "Oh, you have the practical training period, so you can stay longer." So the two years turned into seven. But there was always the visa issue lurking, so I never really planned on staying. And eventually, after looking for work for a very long time, I decided that I wasn't interested in just becoming a web monkey, so I thought I'd go back to London and see what might transpire. But, as I said, once I got there, it seemed that unless I was willing to tie myself to a desk five days a week, nobody was interested. And I had quite a bit of trouble finding work. I was teaching at the London College of Printing one day a week and studying on this course at Reading a couple of days a week too.

What was the product from that?
A typeface that still isn't finished [*Protocol*, completed in Spring 2003] and a dissertation about the Euro currency symbol, which has since found a wider audience in the pages of *Baseline* magazine.

Swedish, 18/24 ▸ Enär er
av det innebo
värdet HOS /
MEDLEMMAI
AV MÄNNISK(
OCH AV deras
lika och oföry
rättigheter är

Swahili, 14/18 ▸ Kwa kuwa
kukiri heshima y
asili na HAKI SA
NA BINADAMU \
NDIO MSINGI W/
UHURU, HAKI NA
AMANI DUNIANI, I
kuwa kutojali na k
haki za binadamu
kumeleta vitendo

Spanish, 12/15 ▸ Considera
que la libertad, la ju
y la paz en el mund
tienen por BASE EL
RECONOCIMIENTO
DE LA DIGNIDAD IN
Y DE LOS DERECHOS
IGUALES E INALIENA
DE TODOS los miem
de la familia human
considerando que el
y el menosprecio de l

Portuguese, 11/14 ▸ Considera
que o reconheciment
da dignidade inerent
a todos os MEMBROS
DA FAMÍLIA HUMAN
E DE SEUS DIREITOS
IGUAIS E INALIENÁVE
É O FUNDAMENTO DA
LIBERDADE, da justiça
e da paz no mundo, con
que o desprêzo e o desr
pelos direitos do home
resultaram em atos bá

Latin, 10/13 ▸ Quoniam conf
est nobis omnes homin
dignitatem mereri et iu
omnium aequata sempi
esse debere, QUIBUS F
LIBERTAS IUSTITIA PA
PER OMNES GENTES C
SINT, QUONIAM QUI IUR
HOMINUM NEGLEGUNT
ET CONTEMNUNT, fas or
ita abrumpunt ut nihil fc
praetermittant et omner
humanitatem exuant, qu
omnes maxime desideran

Italian, 9/11 ▸ Considerato ch
il riconoscimento della di
inerente a tutti membri c
famiglia umana, E DEI LO
DIRITTI, UGUALI ED INAL
COSTITUISCE IL FONDAM
DELLA LIBERTÀ, DELLA C
E DELLA PACE NEL MON
CONSIDERATO CHE IL DISC
E IL DISPREZZO DEI DIRITTI
DELL'UOMO HANNO PORTA
AD ATTI di barbarie che off
la coscienza dell'umanità, e
che l'avvento di un mondo i
cui gli esseri umani godano
della libertà di parola e di c

German, 8/10 ▸ Da die Anerkenn
der allen Mitgliedern der me
Familie innewohnenden Würc
und ihrer gleichen und UNVE
RECHTE DIE GRUNDLAGE D
FREIHEIT, DER GERECHTIGK
UND DES FRIEDENS IN DER
BILDET, DA VERKENNUNG UN
MISSACHTUNG DER MENSCHE
ZU AKTEN DER BARBAREI FÜH
DIE DAS GEWISSEN DER MENS
TIEF VERLETZT HABEN, und da
die Schaffung einer Welt, in de
den Menschen, frei von Furcht
Not, Redeund Glaubensfreiheit
zuteil wird, als das höchste Bes
der Menschheit verkündet worc

French, 7/9 ▸ Considérant que la re
de la dignité inhérent à tous les
de la famille humaine et de leurs
droits égaux et inaliénables cons
le fondement de la liberté, DE LA
JUSTICE ET DE LA PAIX DANS LE
MONDE, CONSIDÉRANT QUE LA
MÉPRIS DES DROITS DE L'HOMM
ONT CONDUIT À DES ACTES DE
BARBARIE QUI RÉVOLTENT LA CON
DE L'HUMANITÉ ET QUE L'AVÉNEM
D'UN MONDE OÙ LES ÊTRES HUMA
SERONT LIBRES DE PARLER ET DE
CROIRE, libérés de la terreur et de l
misère, a été proclamé comme la pl
haute aspiration de l'homme, consi
qu'il est essentiel que les droits de
l'homme soient protégés par un rég
de droit pour que l'homme ne soit p

Finnish, 6/7.5, +1% ▸ Kun ihmiskunna
kaikkien jäsenten luonnollisen arvon
heidän yhtäläisten ja luovuttamattor
oikeuksiensa tunnustaminen on vapa
oikeudenmukaisuuden ja rauhan peru
maailmassa, KUN IHMISOIKEUKSIA C
VÄHEKSYTTY TAI NE ON JÄTETTY H
VAILLE, ON TAPAHTUNUT RAAKALA
JOTKA OVAT JÄRKYTTÄNEET IHMISK
OMAATUNTOA, JA KUN KANSOJEN KO
PÄÄMÄÄRÄKSI ON JULISTETTU SELLAISI
MAAILMAN LUOMINEN, MISSÄ IHMISET
VOIVAT VAPAASTI NAUTTIA sanan ja usk
vapautta sekä elää vapaina pelosta ja pu
kun on välttämätöntä, että ihmisoikeud
turvataan oikeusjärjestyksellä, jotta ihn
ei olisi pakko viimeisenä keinona kapina
pakkovaltaa ja sortoa vastaan, kun on tä
edistää ystävällisten suhteiden kehittyı
kansojen välille, kun Yhdistyneiden Ka
kansat ovat peruskirjassa vahvistane
uskonsa ihmisten perusoikeuksiin, ih
arvoon ja merkitykseen sekä miesten

Dutch, 5/6, +2% ▸ Overwegende, dat erkenn
van de inhaerente waardigheid en van de gel
en onvervreemdbare rechten van alle leden
de mensengemeenschap grondslag is voor de
vrijheid, gerechtigheid en vrede in de wereld
overwegende, dat terzijdestelling van een n
voor de rechten van de mens geleid hebben
barbaarse handelingen, DIE HET GEWETEN
DE MENSHEID GEWELD HEBBEN AANGEDA
EN DAT DE KOMST VAN EEN WERELD, WAA
DE MENSEN VRIJHEID VAN MENINGSUITIN
EN GELOOF ZULLEN GENIETEN, EN VRIJ ZU
ZIJN VAN VREES EN GEBREK, IS VERKONDIG
ALS HET HOOGSTE IDEAAL VAN IEDERE MENS;
OVERWEGENDE, DAT HET VAN HET HOOGSTE B
IS, DAT DE RECHTEN VAN DE MENS BESCHERM
WORDEN, DOOR DE SUPPREMATIE VAN HET RE
opdat de mens niet gedwongen worde om in laa
instantie zijn toevlucht te nemen tot opstand
tyrannie en onderdrukking; overwegende, dat h
van het hoogste belang is, de ontwikkeling van
vriendschappelijke betrekkingen tussen de nati
te bevorderen; overwegende, dat de volkeren va
de Verenigde Naties in het Handvest hun vertro
in de fundamentele rechten van de mens, in de
waardigheid en de waarde van de mens en in
de gelijke rechten van mannen en vrouwen o
hebben bevestigd, en besloten hebben, socia

Type specimen of *Protocol*, designed for Mangat's Master's thesis at Reading University in the UK.

96pt ▸
Protocol is recognisable by a large x-height and carefully constructed form. The (drawn, not sloped) italic is rhythmic without being overtly cursive.

Hlnggaaee

84pt ▸
Protocol's numerals fall somewhere in-between lining and non-lining styles, and are of equal width for simplified tabular setting.

123456789

72pt ▸
Currency symbols complement the figures in height, width, and form. Alternate euro symbols are also included.

$¢£ƒ€€¥

Type specimen of Mangat's *Protocol*, showing variations of letters, numerals and symbols.

So you have a typeface that isn't finished, but what will it be?
It will be a general purpose, humanist sans serif when it's done. Well-trodden ground over the last few years, granted. The Reading course is a Master's Degree in Typeface Design. You look at various technical, historical, and theoretical aspects of type through seminars and lectures, write a few essays, and produce an original typeface and a dissertation.

Is there anything else like it in England or here in North America?
No. The only thing I know of is at the Royal Academy of Art in The Hague — where Just and Erik studied. It's a postgraduate certificate course in type design and typography; the design of text as much as the design of letters themselves.

So Reading's course may be pretty unique...
It's the only one that I know of in the English-speaking world; I've heard conflicting reports as to whether or not the Royal Academy course is taught in English or not. As a university level course though, it's pretty unique, yes.

Do you have a maxim for type design?
I wouldn't really say "maxim" but I do think practicality is one thing I favor. I think — partly because of the capabilities of contemporary type design software — it's become relatively easy to produce enormous type families of multiple widths and weights and sizes and variants. But, as a graphic designer at the other end trying to use them, I find them overwhelming. The software allows it to be done, but is it really needed? Very, very few people need a super family of 144 fonts.

144 fonts within a single type family?!
Yeah, there's all the different weights, and all the different variants. One type of variant that has appeared over the last couple of years is different styles of numeral, so there's a different font for each style of numeral — you'll get lining figures and non-lining, and then proportional and tabular widths ...

So in the end you can have as many as 144?
Oh, there's more than that...

Is this like "super-sizing"?
Yes, exactly, "super families".

That is now a recognized term?
I believe so; there was a French article floating around at Reading which seemed to establish the term "super families."

How do you judge a good typeface?
It is something that is original without being extroverted or appearing to try too hard. It goes back to that Beatrice Warde essay, "The Crystal Goblet or Printing Should Be Invisible," (*The Crystal Goblet, Sixteen Essays on Typography*, Cleveland, 1956). She uses the crystal goblet as a metaphor for clarity, explaining that typography should not get in the way of reading — like a wine glass that doesn't conceal the wine inside it. So it still has to work on a functional level. But it can be original without being overly quirky. Effortless, I guess.

What's functionality then? How do you measure that?
Well there's no real measure.

Is it to do with simplicity of some kind?
How easy it is to read I suppose, how smoothly it flows... and I suppose how easy it is to use for the designer. You can't really ignore the typography either: the appropriateness of the type to the content, the line lengths and spacing, etc.

What's your most popular typeface?
Well, I've only done one... *laughs* That's what always makes me laugh. I'm working on a custom typeface at MetaDesign right now, and I'm actually referred to as a "type designer" but I've only done the one (*Platelet*)...

But you've got the one from Reading that you're nearly done with... and how much is the one that you've done for the Twin Cities typeface project an evolution of that, or other things in the works?
Well the Twin Cities face does look a little similar to *Platelet* in certain ways, but it was entirely original—there was a process leading up to that form. Anyway, I've only got the one commercially available typeface.

How has it sold?
It's done okay, actually. I think it was a case of "right place, right time" quite honestly. No one else was doing monospaced fonts at the time, and now they're all at it.

Does it provide you with beach holidays in the Bahamas?
I get a small check every quarter, which has helped me out on occasion, but it's not enough to live off of by any means. Although it's been one of *Emigre's* best sellers, I'm sure there are others in their "stable" that have done much better.

How do you begin a new type design?
Looking at lots of others, and lots of doodling... People like Erik Spiekermann, Luc(as) de Groot, and Gerard Unger have a very clear skeleton in their minds, which is why their typefaces look so similar. But until I design some more typefaces, I don't really know if I'm the same way.

But you're doing one now at MetaDesign...
Yes, but that's based on an existing typeface.

A typeface that MetaDesign has produced?
No, based on *Trade Gothic* actually.

And how do you pick what you're basing it on?
Well, in this case, it's for a corporate client who's already using *Trade Gothic*, but having problems with the weight and spacing.

What problems did you have to solve and what approaches did you take when working on your *Platelet* typeface? Can you explain where it came from?
Platelet began during a four-day student workshop at CalArts in October '92. The brief from Phil Baines, who led the workshop, asked for an original alphabet to be designed for a specific environment, taking into consideration the context for usage, appropriateness and traditional notions of good typography.

It's based on characters and figures found on car license plates in California. It originally comprised only a single lowercase alphabet and numerals, ostensibly to complement the existing all-caps characters on the plates. For its commercial release through *Emigre*, however, the set was extended to include alternate, small capitals and other commonly used text characters—somewhat ironic considering the original brief had principally been to create specific display faces that weren't just scaled text faces.

Within the short timeframe of the original project, research was limited to quite literally taking wax crayon rubbings from license plates around the parking lot and measuring them by hand. Forms were interpretations of what a lowercase for the license plate might be, based mostly on the existing numerals. As the face developed however, it became necessary to further bold the strokes and stray from the all-lowercase model that had been the conceptual framework to start with; some characters just looked forced.

Do you see uses of *Platelet* that you totally disapprove of?
Since *Platelet* is fairly widely spaced and only has small caps, I'm always seeing it with reduced letterspacing and/or stretched capitals. Or with some sort of weird 'b' to replace the weird 'b' it comes with (even though there's a normal one included in the font anyway). All of which, again, brings up the question of

ABCDEFGHIJKLMNOPQRSTUVWXYZ

abcdefghijklmnopqrstuvwxyz

"0123456789"....'·'

[$¢£f¥]\{?!¿¡}¦(&@%‰#*^)

Thin|Regular|Heavy

ÅÀÂÁÄÃåàâáäãÇçÈÊÉËèêéëÌÎÍÏìîíï

ÑñÒÔÓÖÕØòôóöõøÙÛÚÜùûúüŸÿ

¶§†‡ÆŒæœŒœ•®©™∏π∂µ

°<≤+−÷=≠≈±≥>bfiflß~-–—/

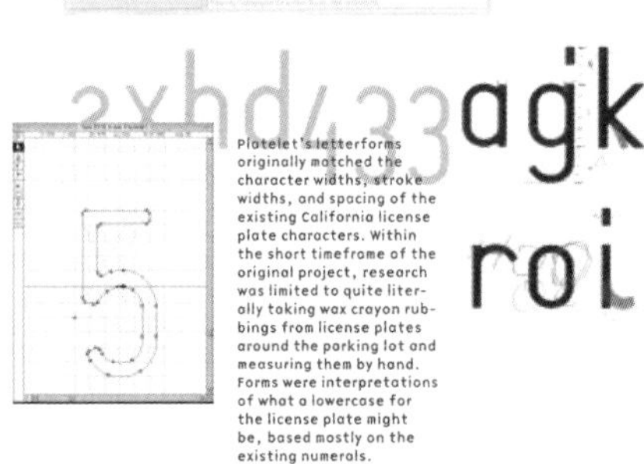

Platelet's letterforms originally matched the character widths, stroke widths, and spacing of the existing California license plate characters. Within the short timeframe of the original project, research was limited to quite literally taking wax crayon rubbings from license plates around the parking lot and measuring them by hand. Forms were interpretations of what a lowercase for the license plate might be, based mostly on the existing numerals.

Platelet also contains some unexpected solutions to the various problems facing monospaced designs, as well as solutions addressing the reduced legibility of geometric designs which have a tendency to render many characters indistinguishable, reducing their function for text applications. The "i" and "l" fill their width not with the standard extended serifs, but with a large curved lead-out stroke. My personal favorite is the lowercase "b" which incorporates the upper case form within the lower case character. This increases the recognition factor of the "b", which would otherwise be very similar to other characters, such as the "d", due to the geometric rigidity of Platelet's letterform construction.

While Platelet is perhaps too fanciful for application on standard license plates, its usage might be suitable for the vanity plates, which the DMV offers at a premium, to further differentiate them from standard plates. The vanity plate owner is allowed to choose a customized arrangement of characters which usually spells a name, word, visual pun, palindrome etc. Since the characters on vanity plates usually have a meaningful arrangement, they are immediately more memorable than a string of random characters, and therefore the design of the letterforms could afford a lesser degree of legibility.

came(r)o

abdegjkqx

abdegjkqx

abdegjkqx

As Platelet developed, it became necessary to bolden the strokes and stray from the all-lowercase model that had been the conceptual framework to start with; some characters just looked forced. A slightly more affected 'unicase' version subsequently developed, dubbed Vanity Platelet.

With a rather awkward marriage of typography and American muscle cars (above) ending nastily, it was clear that all these ideas would be far more successful in a single font. The final family therefore comprised three weights of a single design variant, each with 236 character outlines and four sizes of edited screen fonts.

(Top and bottom): Pages from the specimen book for *Platelet* (1993), originally reproduced in *Platelet: A Typeface Designed by Conor Mangat* ©2001 *Emigre*, Inc.

appropriateness—why not use something similar (but better suited) that doesn't require butchering it to get it to fit? *Platelet* didn't originate as a text face and no amount of abuse will make it into one.

What's the strangest context that you've ever found *Platelet* used?
I don't really document *Platelet* in action, but finding it in 3D neon at an English motorway service station was worthy of a photo. One of my favorite "sightings" was on a "Keep off the Grass" sign in Paris; it just seemed the most bizarre choice. My least favorite are the occasions when someone has passed off what appears to be my work as their own—in products for sale; not clever or flattering, just sad.

"Keep off the Grass" sign in Paris, set in *Platelet*. Photograph by Conor Mangat.

Can a typeface express the particular character of a city?
I'm not sure that it can, without resorting to cliché, that is. A typeface could be a (themed) starting point perhaps; given time, associations might develop that bind the two far more closely than at first. A suitable typeface could become part of a city's architecture (in a broad sense), a constant through time of change. After all, what is a city if not something that is always changing?

What were the challenges you tackled when designing your Twin Cities typeface? For example, were these ideas you had in the back of your mind when the project landed on your desk, or did they come out of something in the brief?
For me, it was a matter of balancing the practical requirements of the brief—a unique and functional typeface for a variety of applications—while leveraging something of the Twin Cities' character and culture. And there's a simple reasoning to this approach: digging too deep can provide meaningless references, while stereotypes—despite the negative associations—can at least provide a common entry point for many viewers. Native American history, Prairie School architecture, the Norwegian influx, Paul Bunyan & Babe, Mary Tyler Moore: I looked at it from a number of angles.

When a local architectural historian commented on how the weather shaped the Twin Cities and their inhabitants, I knew I had the cue I was looking for. Here was something elemental. No obscure stylistic references or complex theories surrounding it; just the universal notions of adversity, positivity and survival. All a bit of a stretch perhaps, but it certainly felt more appropriate than some of the options I just mentioned.

Are there other type designers whom you think are doing interesting work nowadays?
There are, yes, though there's more and more mediocre stuff clouding them too. Matthew Carter continues to stand head and ponytail above us all, of course. And then there's Jonathan Hoefler and Tobias Frere-Jones, with their admirable "armchair history" methodology. Jeremy Tankard's one-man operation is equally admirable, and every time I see a publication from the Royal Academy (in The Hague), I never cease to be amazed by the quality (and quantity) of the work. Talking of which, there's Underware, a Dutch-Finnish studio that I think originated at the Royal Academy. They've put out a couple of very accomplished typefaces in the past couple of years, each accompanied by superbly executed specimen books.

There's also been a significant increase in the discussion of type too, with a number of blogs and forums appearing online. At times it can get a little overwhelming — many of the same people inhabit them all — but the growth in community can only be a good thing.

How do you see the profession and practice of typography/type design changing in the future? Do you think OpenType technology will affect how type designers design?
In much the same way that the desktop PC subsumed all areas of the creative industries in the late Eighties and early Nineties, so too did it make every aspiring type designer truly free of the traditional manufacturing cycle. One could design, produce, promote and deliver all from the same grey box. And one still can, except that the complexity of current fonts (namely, TrueType and OpenType) means that the designer must also be a competent software engineer. And it is here that perhaps we will see a partial split (made narrow by common software tools), with the designer handing final production to an engineer, one who not only knows type but also operating systems and rendering technologies. After all, reading from a screen may be the norm in another ten years.

GILLES GAVILLET & DAVID RUST
OPTIMO
GENEVA & LAUSANNE, SWITZERLAND

Interviewed in Geneva by Deborah Littlejohn
February 8, 2003

"Hopefully, no city can be reduced to a single typeface—except maybe Monaco!"

TwinCitiesDesign2003

Optimo's TCDC typeface proposal, board 1.

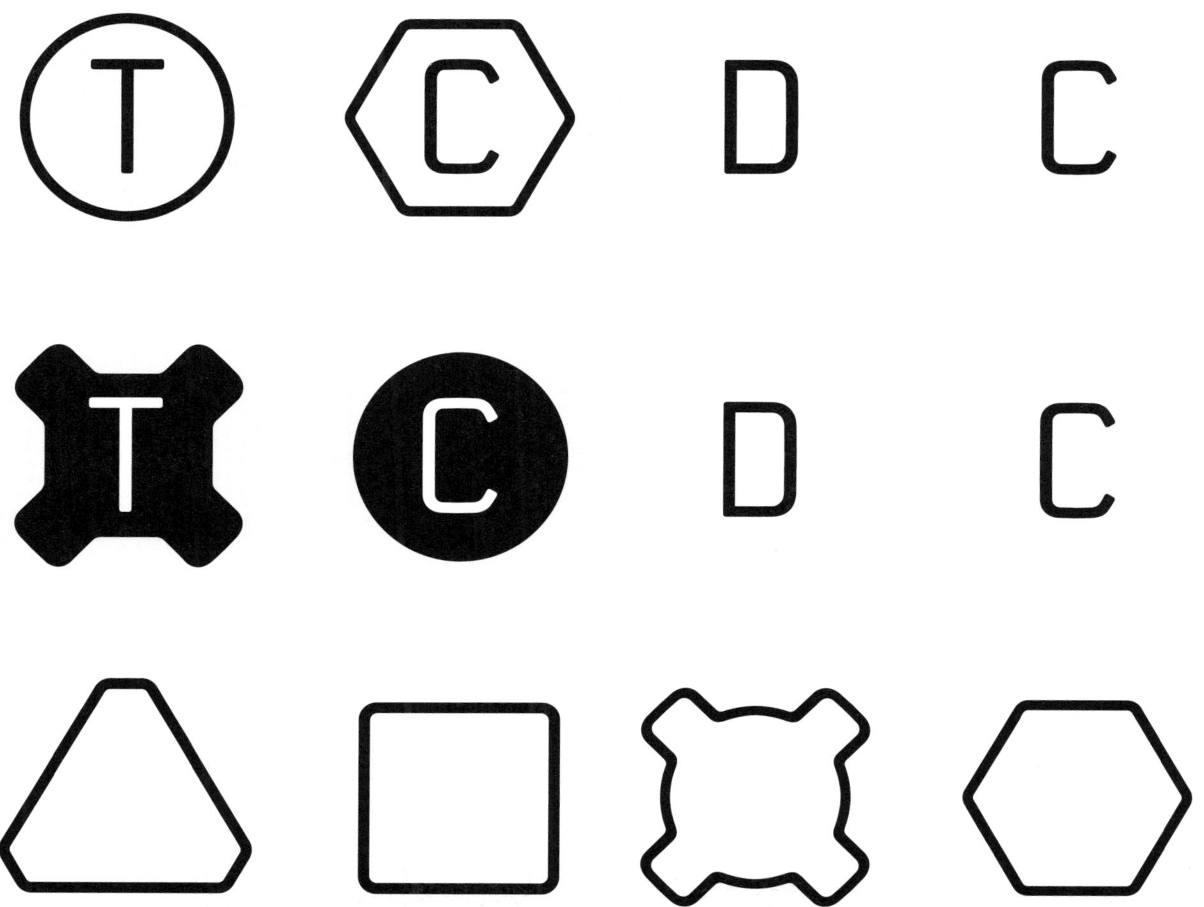

Optimo's TCDC typeface proposal, board 2.

DEBORAH LITTLEJOHN: **Where are you both from originally?**
DAVID RUST: I'm from Switzerland, from Bienna, located at the border between the French and German side.

GILLES GAVILLET: Lausanne, Switzerland.

What is your design background?
GG: We both attended the University of Art and Design in Lausanne, Switzerland in the Visual Communication Department, which offers a five-year program in Graphic Design. While attending art school we established Optimo, (with Stéphane Delgado, who is now working in Paris), as an independent type design label. We started to publish original typefaces through our website in '97. Then I worked for three years with Cornel Windlin at his design studio in Zürich while David was teaching graphic design at the University of Art and Design in Lausanne. In 2001, we reunited forces to continue with Optimo.

DR: The nice thing about the University in Lausanne is that as a part of the design program, it has a strong visiting artist program. The college brings in professional designers from all over the world for short and long-term workshops. While we were students in '95 – '96, we met P. Scott Makela, who was the first visiting designer to start this tradition.

What was your project with the Makelas?
GG: The theme was propaganda. I remember this huge collection of texts Laurie and Scott brought from Cranbrook to start the conceptual development phase of the assignment. Our project in itself wasn't very successful...

DR: It was about genetic engineering and we even used their daughter Carmella as a model for the photography. *laughs* She was photographed looking very insane. Then Scott manipulated her portrait in Photoshop so that she started looking like this weird, cloned child.

GG: Anyway, we had a great time working with Scott. And then later, he and Laurie proposed that we come over and spend some time at Cranbrook Academy of Art where they were the chairs of the 2D Department at the time; they asked David, Stéphane and I to visit.

How did your collaboration as a studio go?
DR: Actually one of the starting points of the collaboration and of the foundry was that stay at Cranbrook. It was the first time we developed a project together.

That was your *Detroit* typeface?
GG: Yes. We had discovered Fontographer software a few months before we left for the U.S., and we were very excited by its potential. We thought that since we weren't staying at Cranbrook for a very long time, it would be nice to give the Makelas and the students something they could keep after we left; to let a little virus loose in the studio. *laughs*

What problems did you have to solve when working on the *Detroit* typeface project? How did you approach this project?
GG: At first, we simply spent a lot of time driving around the city, photographing and filming Woodward Avenue on campus as well as downtown Detroit. Many of the empty buildings downtown (and there have come to be a lot of them recently) had found a new life as "natural" billboards with slogans like "Save Detroit" painted on them. This was one of our starting points. We thought these abandoned houses needed a corporate font.

When we arrived at Cranbrook, multimedia, interactivity and motion graphics were really the "big things" going on in the students' design studio. When we started working on the *Detroit* typeface, it was really funny because the students asked...

DR: ...They asked, "Why are you starting with that kind of thing? Do you really like it?"

It was a MultipleMaster font [see glossary], correct? There were variations between the thick and thin strokes, as well as variations between the round and square joins. Although MultipleMaster is a technology no longer in use today, at the time, wasn't it the "next big thing" in type design?
DR: At the time, yes. Actually we spent a lot of time trying to find out how to make the idea work with the technology. It was a special use of the technology—it wasn't just a MultipleMaster typeface that included infinite choices in weights, so we had to find out how to shape the typeface from "round to square" as well as from "thick to thin" and we had to go through several tests to make sure it would work. We thought that because of its animated quality, it could have nice applications in the motion graphics field.

Do you collaborate on the same projects or are you often working separately between your studios in Geneva and Laussanne?
GG: We do collaborate during the conceptual stages of our projects, at the beginning...

DR: ...But in the end, of course, only one person has the mouse in their hand!

Have you ever considered relocating to another country?
DR: Yes. We have thought about moving to the United States for its size and its relative youth. That has always been an appealing thing to us about the U.S. But where we are now—in Switzerland—is well-situated in the center of the continent and close to everything.

What other projects do you work on besides type design?
GG: We work as a graphic design studio; we design books, posters, catalogues, etc. for commercial and cultural content. Over the past three years we have developed a close collaboration with the book publisher JRP Editions, based here in Geneva.

For us, the cultural sector provides very nice subject matter to work on; and as a type foundry, such projects are a very good field in which to develop and test typefaces; we developed the typeface *Politics* for the catalog *Timewave Zero—the Politics of Ecstasy*, and we designed *Index* as the headline typeface for *Across*, a book analyzing the Swiss art scene over the last 25 years.

How do you begin a new typeface design?
DR: At the beginning it is often a by-product type design—one that comes out of a specific project we are already working on. Developing a special typeface is often a nice way to bring a fresh element to a book or to an identity. Those kinds of projects offer us a chance, as a foundry, to test the type in a real context before releasing it to the public.

The design idea can come from many different sources; for example from an old specimen that we find and want to bring back to life, as we did with the *Hermes* typeface. It is a Sixties Swiss typewriter specimen that we digitized last year. We refined the original drawing and started using it so much that we decided to develop a whole family.

When will your new Website launch [*www.optimo.ch*] and what will be different about it, this go-round?
DR: It will launch in July 2003. It will present the most successful type designs that we have developed over the past three years, as well as a fine selection of other designers' typefaces.

Design-wise, we wanted to propose a very fast and easy way for users to check the fonts, and to be able to see the same typeface in different ways. There will also be a database that will make the whole thing very easy to develop in the future.

What projects are in your studio right now?
GG: Different things—we are just now finishing

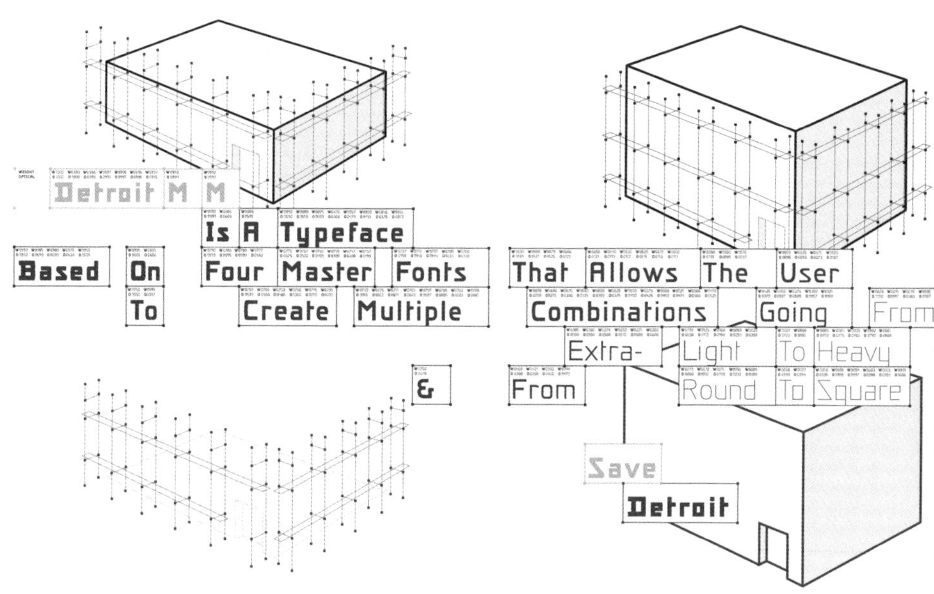

Type specimen of *Detroit* (1997), Optimo's MultipleMaster font, designed while visiting Cranbrook in Bloomfield Hills, MI.

Cargo

ABCMN6RS!
astzkeit@

Hermes

ABCMN6RS!
astzkeit?@

Politics

ABCMN6RS!
astzkeit?@

Optimo typefaces *Cargo* (2002–03), *Hermes* (2002–03, and *Politics* (2001).

up the design of two books: one is for the Biennale of Graphic Arts in Ljubljana, Slovenia, that will take place over the summer; the second book is a monograph for Olivier Mosset, a Swiss artist who is based in Tucson, Arizona, for a big exhibition that will travel to different museums in Switzerland. Then we have to take care of the entire communications and identity design for a photography school in Switzerland.

What is the strangest context in which you've ever found your type designs?
DR: It was in a political context. The square version of *Detroit* was used on a poster that employed a neo-Nazi aesthetic in order to denounce a Swiss politician.

Do you have a maxim for type design?
GG: "The world is written; still, it is necessary to be able to read it."

How do you judge a good typeface?
DR: First on the level of the idea, then we check the technique!

Which is your most popular typeface?
DR: *Detroit* was popular in the Nineties. Right now the *Hermes* typeface is experiencing some nice success, as is *Cargo*, an American template typeface we designed for a few recent projects.

Do you see uses of your fonts that you totally disapprove of?
GG: No: it is the nice part of the game to develop something that will have its own independent life. It is often funny to see how people will appropriate one's type design.

So, can a typeface speak to what is unique about a city?
GG: Hopefully no city's particularity can be reduced to a single typeface—except Monaco!

What were the challenges you tackled when designing your Twin Cities font?
DR: With the TCDC project, we wanted to give the Design Institute a typeface that could embody all the content communicated during the event—from tag lines and headlines to captions and details. So rather than design a font for display use only, we took the text type option—a typeface that could be used in any position in the hierarchy for communications materials. We tried to produce something whose basic aesthetic would relate to urban reports or geographic maps. Then we developed another layer to the font by designing a set of signs or marks that brought into the font a new typology that came from the public domain; road signs, building signage, etc...

Should the general public care about type design?
GG: Our everyday visual environment is literally strewn with words; from newspapers to food packaging; from utilitarian objects to clothes; from vehicles to buildings; people pass through a continuous forest of signs. Make no mistake—its permeability is only the other side of your own. By traveling through the everday environment, everybody is pierced by these "bundled rays" of trademarks, visual identities, imprints, and images.

DR: Typography is therefore present at all times and at all everyday locations. Being one of the primary means by which words are made, typography participates in the definition of an ambience, and of an exchange. By playing here on coincidence, there on rupture, on the evident or on the slippage of transparency or opacity, typography makes fissures in the way a word functions.

GG: Television provides good terrain for observing these propositions. On the news channels, for example, a line of text sliding across the screen beneath the image window has gradually become commonplace. Starting at CNN and NBC, it is now becoming the international television norm. This concept of heterogeneous information strata, some iconic and others textual, is linked to another phenomenon: the *becoming-image* and incidentally the *becoming-logo* of dramatic events taking place over time. So we've seen ever more sophisticated staging of "the news" during the recent armed conflicts involving the United States. Every time, these wars that we also know to be media wars came with a particular system of image management and, in that context, were decked out in logos that would not have dishonored the poster displays of movie houses or Hollywood ads.

DR: At the 1998 Berlin Biennale, a cross-disciplinary symposium drew attention to a unique example of the role typographic design plays in social and political discourse and the latter's effect on daily life. The city of Berlin had given Erik Spiekermann's MetaDesign the assignment of producing a new visual identity for the city. Lionel Bovier brought together a number of experts to discuss this strategy and its implications. The discussion dealt both with the choice of the ambiguous symbol of the Brandenburg Gate to represent a city in full reconstruction, and with the very principle of considering the city as a kind of firm that one could try and "sell" through its image, building the future through its representations. Today, the near bankruptcy of Berlin leaves little doubt as to the limitations of selling a city with a purely visual identity.

GG: In Minneapolis itself, another example comes to mind: in '92 or '93, didn't the singer then still known by the name of Prince try to become a symbol, a "love symbol"? We would gladly have advised this "man-sign" to pick some good typography as a logo, rather than a mere dingbat! (laughs)

How do you see the profession and practice of type design changing in the future?

DR: The big change was during the Nineties when the technology, typefaces and software became more accessible to graphic designers—not just type designers—including its delivery through the Internet. Looking at the actual evolution of software, it might move back into the hands of the specialists as it's becoming more and more complex on the technical level.

Are there other type designers whom you think are doing interesting work nowadays?

GG: We like the work of our friends Cornel Windlin and Stefan Mueller from Lineto.

What new Optimo typeface creation can we look forward to in the future?

DR: A typeface called *Holidays*, inspired by a Sixties California text type we photographed in Los Angeles last winter—while on holiday!

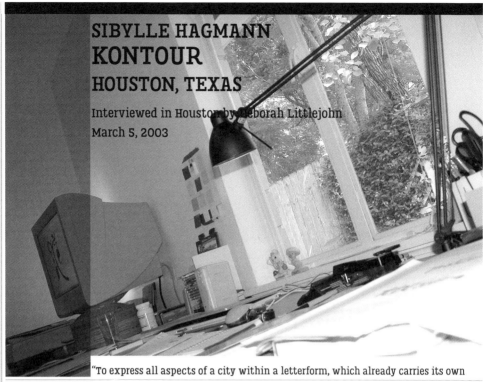

SIBYLLE HAGMANN
KONTOUR
HOUSTON, TEXAS

Interviewed in Houston by Deborah Littlejohn
March 5, 2003

"To express all aspects of a city within a letterform, which already carries its own message, is perhaps impossible to achieve."

24 points Twin Cities Design 2003

72 points Twin Cities Design 2003

42 points Twin Cities Design Celebration 2003

Sibylle Hagmann: TCDC typeface proposal, board 1.

Twin Cities

Twin Cities Text Regular

Twin Cities

St. Paul Thin Script

Twin Cities

Minneapolis Super Bold

Twin Cities Elements

Sibylle Hagmann: TCDC typeface proposal, board 2.

ABCDEFGHIJKLMNOPQRSTU
VWXYZabcdefghijklmnopqrst
uvwxyz.,:;?!“”’0123456789

8/10

The Twin Cities is noted for its array of intriguing theater, fine orchestras, art museums ar
garden. There's always a full calendar of visiting performers and Broadway touring shows
Interesting museums, professional sports, riverboats and a variety of nightspots add to t
the Twin Cities. Along the Mississippi riverfront in Minneapolis are historic mills, the 1883
Bridge, and scenic walkways. Downtown St. Paul is home to a creative children's museum,
science museum and landmark history center. Not surprisingly, water-based activities are
the "Land of 10,000 Lakes." Minnesota is home to the largest lake (Superior) in the world,
acre Boundary Waters Canoe Area Wilderness, the crystal-clear source of America's might
and vast portions of the state are carpeted by countless lakes, streams, rivers, and forest
green and hardwood.

12/16

The Twin Cities is noted for its array of intriguing theater, fi
orchestras, art museums and a sculpture garden. There's alw
full calendar of visiting performers and Broadway touring sl
as well. Interesting museums, professional sports, riverboat
variety of nightspots add to the appeal of the Twin Cities. Al
Mississippi riverfront in Minneapolis are historic mills, the 1
Stone Arch Bridge, and scenic walkways. Downtown St. Paul
home to a creative children's museum, top-notch science mu
and landmark history center. Not surprisingly, water-based
ties are a big draw in the "Land of 10,000 Lakes." Minnesota
home to the largest lake (Superior) in the world, the million-
Boundary Waters Canoe Area Wilderness, the crystal-clear s
of America's mighty Mississippi, and vast portions of the sta

24/27

The Twin Cities is noted for its
intriguing theater, fine orches
museums and a sculpture gard
There's always a full calendar
ing performers and Broadway
shows, as well. Interesting mu

Sibylle Hagmann: TCDC typeface proposal, board 3.

Sibylle Hagmann: TCDC typeface proposal, board 4.

DEBORAH LITTLEJOHN: You are originally from Switzerland, you attended design school in Basel, and then later moved to the U.S. and received an MFA in California at CalArts. Now you live in Houston where you founded a design and typography practice. Do you consider yourself a Swiss designer or an American designer? Or do you think such distinctions are not important anymore?

SIBYLLE HAGMANN: I don't consider myself as being a Swiss or American designer, but rather someone whose creative decisions happen to be influenced and formed by the different dogmas of education she passed through. National distinctions show most when comparing educational approaches—which are influenced by tradition, society and a political past and present. But even those differences seem to diminish as global connectivity contributes to the blurring of typical regional characteristics. Since we have the chance to see what other designers are doing, no matter where they are doing it, our actions are in constant flux. I have a feeling that I'm most influenced by my immediate environment, though. At the moment this happens to be Houston, and on a more important and larger scale, the U.S.

What do you most identify with in Houston?

My partner is a neuroscientist and our decision to move to Houston was motivated by his work. Since we have only been here a little more than two years, I haven't yet discovered the city in all its details. My car doesn't wear an "Eat more Beef" bumper sticker, *laughs* but I probably most identify with Houston's size and international community. What I miss most from California are the mountains and the outdoors. The humidity and heat during the summer here seem to make shopping malls an appealing alternative for many people. I have never seen a higher concentration of malls than here, and I'll bet that Houston would even beat Southern California in this regard! There are only a few widely esteemed art museums in Houston; one of my favorites is the Menil Collection.

Have you ever considered setting up shop in another city or country?

Oh, yes. So far, the choice of where to live and work is a result of me wanting to attend a certain institution, or wanting to harmonize my professional life with my husband's. We are not very bound to one particular city or country. I see relocating as a challenge, one that is usually filled with opportunities. But I always felt more at ease with the idea of setting up a studio here in the U.S. than with doing so in Europe, and in particular in Switzerland. Things can be complicated in very small countries.

What impact has the vibe or ambience of each city where you've studied and lived had on your approach to design?

My actions are influenced by the environment I live in, but more importantly, perhaps, by the people I am in contact with. I hold dear the places that helped me to develop and unfold personally and professionally—most important in this regard is Los Angeles, where I studied and lived for seven years and met many interesting people, who also became friends. Los Angeles' ambience, bewitched by a mixture of stardom, multi-culturalism and smog, very directly influenced my approach to design. Zürich, where I worked in the design studio Eclat before moving to the U.S., was also an important place for me. Other factors influencing my approach to design are the availability of urban resources. I enjoy being inspired by an eclectic palette of cultural and intellectual stimuli, such as the opportunity to see films untouched by Hollywood, bookstores stacked with a rich selection of design, art and architecture books, and good museums, among several other things.

Do you have a "maxim" for type design?

Never leave any idea untested and keep the mind open in the process.

How do you judge a good typeface?

A good typeface radiates optical harmony. The

different parts are in perfect accord with each other and the appearance doesn't convey the pain and suffering it cost the designer to create the characters! It also seems to me that a good typeface is a riddle solved successfully, like forensic work—finding the right puzzle pieces that fit together. But of course, the quality of a typeface also depends on its intended use, cultural perceptions and changing technologies.

What do you mean by "pain and suffering"?
I was thinking about two things: the creative process, which consists of wrestling with decisions about form, and so on; and the diligence required to complete an entire character set. I'm not easily satisfied with the work I produce. I force myself to question the results, and to approach the problem from as many different perspectives as possible. To develop appropriate, working results, I try to fail as early in the process as possible. Unfortunately, we are taught that failure is bad. I believe that failures ultimately make us more creative. The eventual goal, of course, is to succeed. But to develop unique ideas, it takes a familiarity with failure and a willingness to fall short. This goes hand-in-hand with questioning and selectively rejecting established rules, standards and dogmas so that experiments can continue.

What made you decide to design typefaces?
Mainly a frustration with the commercial aspects of graphic design. I have a hard time complying with a client's "graphically incorrect" requests, and I never liked the service side of the profession. Partly out of this dissatisfaction, I attended graduate school to find out whether I wanted to continue working in the field of graphic design or not. Luckily, during the two years of graduate study, I re-discovered typography and type design. It became a niche activity with a creative freedom I enjoyed a lot. Up until now, most of the type design projects I have worked on are self-imposed studies. So the nature of this activity is much less influenced by a client's opinion. Within the last couple of years, I have also been able to steer my graphic design work more towards projects I'm truly passionate about. Typography is one of the few subjects within graphic design with a rich and long history.

How do you begin a new typeface design, in general? Can you describe your working methods?
By sketching lowercase letters like 'a,' 'e' or 's'. In the beginning, I'm less concerned about the uppercase. Often there is a detail in a lowercase character that I want to pursue, such as a certain form of serif, or how the curves are modulated. I'm driven to find out whether this detail and specific characteristic could work out in a complete character set. Seeing the letters applied in a paragraph is the next revealing moment. I look at different point sizes of text to judge overall appearance and to see where problems occur. For details such as curves or counter spaces, I print the letters out at a larger scale. I continue the process by using tracing paper and pencil to make corrections, and I work on details by going back and forth between these sketches, and by eyeballing the changes on screen.

How long does it take to design a typeface?
It depends very much on the project. Title fonts normally do not take as long to complete as text fonts do. Text fonts need much more fine tuning and therefore more time to develop. If I'm working on a self-imposed project, it may take me months or even years to design a comprehensive family of typefaces. I also like to store sketches of letters away for some time so I can gain the necessary distance to see more clearly where problems in the design emerge.

Which is your most popular typeface and how would you explain its success?
The font package *Cholla Sans* (*Thin*, *Regular*, *Italic* and *Bold*) is the sub-family (of the 20 cuts available) ordered most often from *Emigre*. It doesn't surprise me — I always felt most con-

fident about *Cholla Sans Regular*, which was developed first. The other weight I personally favor within the family is the *Sans Italic*. The two weights go well together, and each possess their own individual details. The sans members, *Bold* and *Thin*, complete the foursome nicely.

How many typefaces have you designed?
Besides *Cholla*, I designed and completed two other families, each consisting of three weights. Neither of them is commercially distributed and I doubt that they ever will be. The *Cholla* family, which includes around 20 fonts, is the only one commercially available.

What approaches did you take when working on the *Cholla* typeface?
The development was fed by a close collaboration with Denise Gonzales Crisp who was then in charge of the design office at Art Center College of Design in Pasadena, CA, and recognized some potential in *Cholla*. Due to a very fruitful collaboration the family grew to the many weights it has.

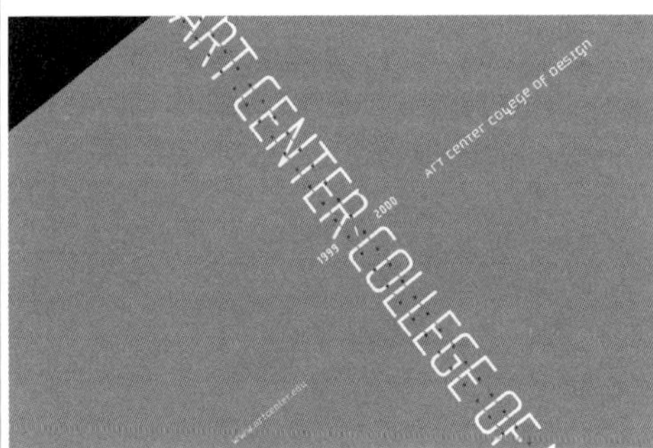

Cholla on the cover of Art Center's catalog, designed by Denise Gonzales Crisp in 1999. Image courtesy Sibylle Hagmann.

Denise and I were classmates during grad school at CalArts. Shortly before we graduated, I started sketching what later became the regular sans weight of *Cholla*. I kept working on it, and Denise followed its progress with some interest. I was going back to work in design when she became the art director of Art Center's design office. For the *1999–2000 Admissions Catalogue*, it was her vision to use typefaces which weren't yet commercially released—*Cholla Regular* was one of them. As the font was put into use, additional weights were commissioned. *Regular Sans Italic* was worked out, and Denise, together with associate designer Carla Figueroa, expressed interest in a light, and later, a bold cut. Over a relatively short period of time, we created a series of fonts that would offer a great deal of variation. The variety was needed in order to echo the school's nine different departments, yet together, the fonts had to exude a unified feel.

Stylistically, the 12 cuts have slightly different personalities, with different ideas applied. For example, the bold weight isn't simply the regular with weight gain, but has bold letterforms with their own peculiar details. After the different *Cholla* weights, with subfamilies *Regular*, *Slab* and *Wide*, were designed, and the admissions catalogue received positive feedback for its design and typefaces, Denise decided to continue to use the fonts for other Art Center projects. The design office commissioned the font family for exclusive use for some time before the typefaces became available through *Emigre's* foundry.

How can a typeface convey what is special about a city? Or can it?
This is a challenging task. A city is a multifaceted, living organ, containing many contrasting aspects: the ugly and the nice; the old and the new; the stressful and the relaxing; and numerous other influences and conditions such as the weather, or the geographic position. To express or reflect any of these aspects within a letterform, which already carries its own message, is perhaps impossible to achieve. One possible approach could be to express the ambience of a city rather than particular aspects of it. But this challenge is for an individual visual translation based on personal experience, best done by someone who has spent an extended time in the city. In the case of my draft for the Twin

Typography has
become the study of placing letter
AaBbCcDdEeFfGgHhIiJjKkLlMmNnOoPpQqRrSsTtUuVvWwXxY

Typography has
become the study of placing letter
AaBbCcDdEeFfGgHhIiJjKkLlMmNnOoPpQqRrSsTtUuVvWwXxY

TYPOGRAPHY HA
BECOME THE STUDY OF PLACING LE
AABBCCDDEEFFGGHHIIJJKKLLMMNNOOPPQQRRSSTTUUVVWWX

Typography has
become the study of placing letter
AaBbCcDdEeFfGgHhIiJjKkLlMmNnOoPpQqRrSsTtUuVvWw

The Typography
A VIEW OF FONT DESIGN

ABCDEFGHIJKLMNOPQRSTUVWXYZABFHIJLRSTVWY

Type specimen of Hagmann's in-process typeface *Odile*.

Cities principal font, I tried to translate the perspective view of streets and building roof lines receding into the distance, and to create an illusion of a three-dimensional space, conveyed in the angles of the inside of a room on a two-dimensional surface.

In order to reflect the diversity of Twin Cities streetscapes, I suggested an echo of architectural variety in the vernacular font weights, all based on the same skeletal structure and form principals as the main font. These vernacular fonts—formally reminiscent of architectural characteristics such as a Victorian, turn-of-the-century form-language and details—and a bold weight that reflects the strong and massive presence of skyscrapers and high rises, could have been developed to become interpolated intermediate weights.

Were these ideas you were already working on when the project landed on your desk, or did they come out of something in the brief?
I didn't start out with any preconceived ideas since I lacked a close familiarity with the Twin Cities. I had visited Minneapolis before, which gave me a small idea about the place, but certainly not enough to have some readymade ideas. The formal outcome was rooted mainly in researching the Twin Cities online and from books. One of the main challenges was that the brief called for flexible and manifold applications of the typeface, such as the generation of a logotype, as well as text for printed documents, and for onscreen usage, among others. This became especially tricky since the face's design also had to be recognizable as unique.

Do you teach typography?
Currently I teach full time at the University of Houston in the Communications department. I taught before at Art Center among other institutions. When I teach I see myself in the role of a coach, someone who encourages and passes on a passion for the subject. One of the most gratifying things about teaching is to see the students falling in love with design, form, concept, idea and type throughout the course of a semester. My goal is to support each individual student's experience as opposed to preaching dogmatic ideas. For this reason, each student's final solution to a given design problem can look very different.

How has the teaching of typography changed since you studied it, and now teach it? Is it different in the U.S., compared to Basel, where you studied?
I'm not sure if the teaching of typography can be separated from how the teaching of graphic design has changed over the last couple of decades in the U.S. As graphic design established itself as a subject to study at colleges and universities and moved away from the realm of the more commercial "graphic art," so did typography. Because of technological changes, such as the introduction of the PC, designers have gained much more direct access to typography. Type no longer needs to be ordered from the typesetting bureau, and a range of font styles can be tested instantaneously. This fact perhaps led to a heightened awareness of what role type design plays within graphic design, which may have led to typography being given a more prominent position in schools' curricula.

The teaching of typography at the Basel School of Design was very much following the dogmatic and rigid Swiss typography rules established by Emil Ruder and Josef Mueller-Brockmann. Students were encouraged to work with Adrian Frutiger's *Univers Condensed*, almost no matter what the assignment was about. I can't remember having ever used a serif typeface for a project. When I graduated from Basel in '89, the school had just purchased its first Macs, and designers and students were about to make the shift from traditional tools to digital tools. Overall, my sense is that typography in the U.S. was also influenced by other professional practices, such as advertising and commercial lettering which concentrated perhaps less on century-old typographic traditions. This multi-focused approach may have created a diversity and richness within typography not found in a more reserved and conservative Europe.

How do you see the profession and practice of typography and type design changing in the future? Will the emerging OpenType technology affect how type designers design fonts?
Now that the technology-driven type design frenzy of the Nineties has somewhat calmed itself, designing letters seems to have gone back again into the hands of more established and perhaps more trained people. This trend will be strengthened as technology becomes progressively more complex. At the same time, advancing technology gives users of typography more control over matters that were previously inaccessible; for example, thanks to current software, designers can instantaneously test different typefaces used in their projects, or even digitally manipulate letterforms to their own liking.

Technology offers new methods of inventing form. While I would much rather keep focusing on designing fonts, the individual and independent type designer cannot get around the problem of dealing with yet more new type formats. OpenType will present new possibilities and be food for fresh thought and ideas. Though it is a new format and not a design tool, it will still affect how type designers design. One of the advantages of OpenType is that the user can work with a huge character set, as opposed to sets which are split up into single expert fonts. It isn't supported by many software programs yet, so we will see how fast the format will establish itself, and if it can stand the test of time. These days, layout programs are able to fix badly-kerned and spaced type as well as ill-looking typography. There the question becomes, "will we no longer need to teach the 'do's' and 'don'ts' of typography?"

How does your studio function, day-to-day?
Two things that pretty much define how my studio functions are my teaching commitment, and the fact that I'm the sole employee. Teaching takes approximately half, or more, of my week. Teaching allows me to be picky about the kind of work and clients I want to work for.

Did you make a conscious decision to stay a one-woman operation? Have you ever thought about expanding your studio?
Yes, it is a conscious decision. After working in different kinds of settings, such as small studios consisting of a maximum of three people, to large agencies with 150 employees, I came to the conclusion that I wanted to be on my own. I'm convinced that the size of my operation gives me some of the creative freedom I yearn for. This does not exclude collaborations of any kind.

Are there other type designers whom you think are doing interesting work nowadays?
Studying other type designers' work is captivating. It can be interesting in many different ways: classical-looking work fascinates me because of the level of quality that can be achieved. Letterform experimentations may convince me because of the persuasive power of new ideas, or the use of new technologies. Of course, one doesn't exclude the other. I find that there are many individual and independent type designers who are doing interesting work, yet it's just a handful of people whose work and names I keep stumbling over. Let's hope for some newcomers, including females.

Why do you think there are so few well-known women type designers?
One might think that women are more easily intimidated by technology, but today there are more female graphic designers than males working in a profession where technology plays a major role. Type design, in most cases, focuses on the anatomy of lines. Could it be that designing letters seems to be a cold,

black-and-white activity without images or colors? Another reason may be that there aren't too many institutions in the world offering an education in type design. And independent of gender, I wonder how many type designers are out there truly making a living from the sole activity of type design?

Who are some of the women type designers you most admire?
There are so few, but Zuzana Licko [co-founder with Rudy VanderLans at *Emigre*] is certainly one of them.

What new Sibylle Hagmann typeface can we look forward to in the future?
I'm working on a small serif family, called *Odile*, which at this point is still in its early phase. The conceptual ideas are laid out, but there are hundreds of details still in question. The inspiration came from an experimental typeface, *Charter*, designed by W. A. Dwiggins around 1937. Only the lowercase was made and the typeface was never released. *Charter* was informal in its shape, upright, and suggestive of script, though the letters didn't join. I'm hoping to have the family, which currently consists of five weights, ready for distribution sometime in the near future. Conceptually, *Odile's Regular* and *Special* uppercases can be applied with different lowercase weights of the family. This could be a project for the new OpenType format.

ERIK VAN BLOKLAND & JUST VAN ROSSUM
LETTERROR
THE HAGUE & HAARLEM, THE NETHERLANDS

Interviewed in Haarlem by Deborah Littlejohn

February 6, 2003

“The most obvious way, which is also the most horrible way, would be to get some graphic element of the place into the shapes of the letters…and it’s just kitsch.”

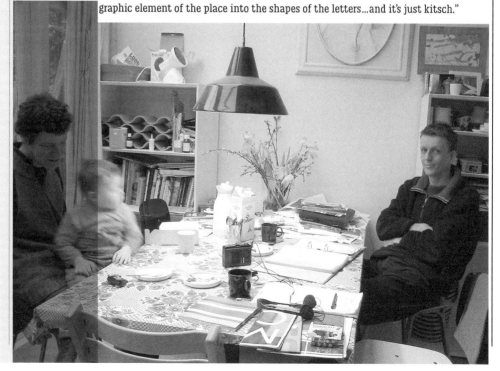

Type and Cities

This is Panel 1

A Style?

Is it possible to match any particular typographic style with a city? The streets and buildings don't care for one typeface or the other. But the people that live in the city might. If the city is big you will find opinions and preferences about anything. Is it possible to please a majority of citizens ? It's already difficult to choose a typeface from the current selection, it makes it near impossible to please everybody when designing a new one.

First you need to address the matrix of possible applications. Do you want to use the typeface on screen? *yeah sure*, on newsprint? *of course!* on building size billboards? *why not!* Then you need to multiply this matrix with the wide range of preferences you'll find in the city's population. *Traditional! modern! postmodern! funky!*, "fast" and the classic "just like the type on TV" to make it look like the design of the latest popular sitcom. And all that preferably in just *one* font.

The traditional approach in a problem like the Twin City typeface would be to draw several styles that would loosely fit together. A sans and a serif with matching italics for both. Bound to please a few people and look acceptable to the rest. It's a sure way to get rather traditional results: good, but not particularly different from the rest. But if you stray too far from the typographic middle ground an increasing number of people will criticize the design.

Adding styles to the typeface is only a partial solution. Each additional weight makes it more difficult to choose the right one. Despite the current trend in typedesign to build larger and larger families: *more is not always better.*

The Alternator!

Over the years at LettError we have been working on various methods to add stylistic variations to type (Beowolf, Kosmik, Bitpull). The new solution, invented for this occasion and presented here, is named *The Panchromatic Hybric Style Alternator.* The alternator focusses on the different groups of shapes in the western alphabet and how they are distributed: *curves, stems, serifs and contrast.* Not all letters have serifs: the lowercase 'o' for instance. Not all letters have curves, not all letters show contrast. Rather than making full sets of letters for each desired style, the Alternator starts with *one single alphabet* of appropriate weight and width.

The fun starts with applying the alternates in text and typography. When the typeface is delivered by *LetterSetter* (www.lettersetter.com) or as an *OpenType* typeface, complex rules of selecting alternates can be applied without bothering the user. Alternates can be selected based on the *context*, for instance: take this version of 'e' when it is preceded by 'h'. The Alternator controls which alternates are used and how often shapes of a specific 'flavor' appear in the text. Thus the overall appearance can be tuned to different tastes for different applications.

A type system based on the Alternator method offers great flexibility. Alternator type brings a very particular flavoring to the resulting text: useful for logotypes and headlines, but it can be quiet and behave like a normal typeface. The type designers basically build a machine with which the users of the system can fool around. This gives the users the control to decide which set of Alternator values is appropriate for a specific job. It's as if the typeface consists of hundreds of styles, but without the massive font menu.

st paul'

LettError Twin City Type Proposal, © 2002, WR LettError

LettError's TCDC typeface proposal, board 1.

This is Panel (2)

But How?

The TCDC Alternator can have several dimensions or parameters. Each parameter has a range of values it can be set to and controls a specific characteristic in the text. Some parameters affect all letters, others control the way certain alternates are distributed. Note that this is a fundamentally different approach than *"multiple master fonts"*. The borderline between typedesign and typography is blurring in the Alternator system. The user (typographer, graphic designer) gets more control over issues previously left to the typedesigner. In return the typedesigner gets more control over typography.

St. Pauls stuffed gaffe

EƐeosPleased

EƐee

A lower contrast between the thick and thin strokes makes it easier for alternative shapes to blend in.

qqq nnnr

Pahigila

qq:q nnnńn

qqq

Tgwxo

Technical

At the moment, Alternator type can be delivered in three different systems. The most flexible and at the same time easiest to maintain and control is as a *LetterSetter* application. LetterSetter is our on-line outline factory, currently in use as a font previewer for our typecollection. But LetterSetter can produce cross platform PDF documents as well. Play with the controls until the logotype is what you want, then download the PDF for printing or further editing. A LetterSetter system for the TCDC can deliver 'authorized' logotypes to any number of users who get to submit their own content, text, names etc. The LetterSetter engine will translate the wishes and content in the proper manner, apply all the rules we've made up for selecting alternates and even use the right colors. The users receive high-resolution artwork that works in all major graphics applications without having to deal with and install complicated font families.

The second option for Alternator type is *OpenType* is a new font format developed by Adobe and Microsoft. It is not as flexible as LetterSetter, but OpenType fonts can do some magic all by themselves. Contextual glyph substitution and large sophisticated charactersets to name a few.

LettError's TCDC typeface proposal, board 2.

EƐ·aɑ·g·Fff·ji·pɲ·Ss·lL·qQ

St. Ɛden qualified

Social quants eat justified liberties stern Et

Ɛchos Erstnile Public Footɲath rednecia Fs.

danish tipografed lettƐrror ijsje eten. Eh.

En hard roepen hoe daar is lars en Paul. naar die luisteren natuurlijc helenaal niet. bel naar dus.

ƐEFPS·aɑbcdeffghijjlLnopɲqQrstu·

Shape

The challenge is first to draw shapes that are different in construction, but do not disturb the overall color and rythm of the text. And then to define the context in which the shapes would appear.

We start by carefully choosing a contrast (the difference between the thick and thin parts of the lettershape). A medium contrast that allows both sans and serif constructions. Angular and curved forms for the bowls would mix as well. Then we need to make a table of alternate constructions for each letter.

The outlines would not be jaggy as these sketches show but have a more formal and smooth surface. The construction would have both formal and informal qualities distributed over the alternates.

Conclusion

We believe that the Alternator system would bring the diversity and liveliness that is needed in a type system that is to reflect the twin cities. The TCDC problem requires a broader approach than finding the right serif for Minneapolis or the curve which expresses the character of St. Paul. The Alternator can address more typographic problems than regular fonts and solve them in a unique way.

We're convinced that the results will be pleasing and recognisable but also have a particular voice that will set the TCDC typography apart from the rest. We also recognise that the alternator is an *unusual solution, untested design ideas and experimental technology*. But this is the way that we have always approached design problems – technology is there to serve design and typography. Make the most of it.

Early sketches of alternative constructions and forms. In detail the variations continue: some stroke end round and other straight. The lowercase 'g' stems from Denmark. The capheight is very low. Alternates with different stem heights are an option.

alternate construction, same contrast

LettError Twin City Type Proposal, © 2002, LettError

LettError's TCDC typeface proposal, board 3.

DEBORAH LITTLEJOHN: **Where are you both from originally?**
ERIK VAN BLOKLAND: I am from Gouda, Holland.

JUST VAN ROSSUM: I am from here, Haarlem.

You live and work here?
JVR: Yeah. Well, I lived in The Hague for a long time before now, so it's only fairly recently that I moved here.

So, you do graphic design and typography, programming, and animation — do you consider yourself designers, typographers, programmers, or all of these things?
JVR: Many of these things.

EVB: Yes, but we don't have business cards with these titles on them. I think we just accept whatever commissions or assignments we can get, and see if we can reasonably make it work. Mainly it's type and typography, but we've done other things as well.

What about the animations? [see TypoMan *http://www.letterror.com/projects/typoman*]
JVR: Yes, well that started mainly as a hobby project with Erik.

EVB: I do a bit of illustration, and animation is just the next step up.

JVR: You were making drawings before you went to art school, so you've been making illustrations longer than you've been drawing type.

EVB: That's true.

JVR: So, yeah, with respect to programming it's usually still fairly close to our typography and type. Type-related tools.

Do both of you program software?
EVB: Yes, well, Just on a University level and me on, like, a high school level... *laughs*

Did either of you study computer science?
EVB AND JVR: No no no!

JVR: It started as a hobby, but there are times that I actually like it more than doing design, so I've educated myself over the past few years.

Do you think at this time — when everything is so specialized — that there's something unique about design in that it lets someone pursue all of these different kinds of practices?
JVR: I don't think we started programming to be unique. It was basically an acquired skill that turned out to be very useful.

EVB: Because the tools that were available weren't good enough, and even though programming superficially doesn't have anything to do with design — it looks totally different, with screens of text, abstract and error messages, and documentation...

JVR: ...mostly error messages ... *laughs*

EVB: ...it enables us to come up with new ways of making type, or new ways of making typography, or new ways of making animation...

JVR: Programming came naturally to us. We both independently worked and played with computers before we went to art school, and basically we went to study design because it was something that sounded interesting. But it turned out soon enough that these two things go really well together, and that worked especially well at the time we studied — this was the mid- to late-Eighties —so there were computers, but everything was quite primitive. There were a lot of things to do and a lot of things to experiment with. So I think that today with the current state of software, there might be a lot less need to start programming.

Are there many typographers who use programming in their work?

JVR: We know a few, but it is not really common.

EVB: But, you can include writing action scripts for Flash in your definition of programming too.

JVR: You can call writing HTML programming, and there is Javascript, so there are a lot of designers who deal directly or indirectly with computer programming.

EVB: One of our theories is that programming is a way to either make new tools or to build extensions to existing ones, rather than to conform your ideas to what your programs can do. We build the software to support the ideas.

JVR: With existing software, it is very, very uniquely integrated. We are not really capable of writing a really nice drawing program—that would be a lot of work. We could never reach the levels of quality that Adobe Illustrator has. But still, we often have the need to draw things with Illustrator that Illustrator doesn't let us draw, because what we're asking is simply too complicated. So instead of writing a standalone tool that allows us to do what we want to do, we actually build a bunch of tools that create Adobe Illustrator files, which we can then open in Illustrator and work with manually. That's an example of how some of our tools would work.

EVB: We would not write one programming machine as a solution to everything, but instead we look at all the existing programs, including the stuff that we write on our own. We see what the missing puzzle pieces are, and say "well, we need to go from here to there... and we can either take this way, we can take that way, or we can build a bridge from here to this, to that or..."

But you also distribute your software; you're building tools for designers as well?
JVR: To an extent. I mean we have our RoboFog tool which is interesting to a fairly specialized group of type designers. And we've actually managed to convert a bunch of type designers to become—well, not to become programmers, but to become proficient enough in programming that they can actually use Robofog and add tools to it to fit their own needs.

EVB: We can write the software, we can license it to maybe, thirty, forty, fifty people. But it is not the case that, you know, we have engineers working for us in the programming department, and shrink-wrapping and manuals, and all that stuff.

Oh, yes, the side industry. *laughs*
JVR: Marketing.

EVB: Marketing.

Technical support... *laughs*
EVB: Technical Support.

JVR: No technical support...

How did you decide that you would work together and then name yourselves LettError?
EVB: That happened separately. The LettError name actually was suggested by Just when I had a small type-focused magazine at the Royal Academy in The Hague. And I didn't have any name, and Just suggested "Letterreur", but later we internationalized that into LettError.

JVR: We weren't in the same class, but we were in the same school. We were one year apart, and being relatively young nerds who didn't socialize, well, we knew of each other's existence.

EVB: Hey, I had friends....

JVR: I had friends too...except you weren't one of them!

EVB: ...and for good reason...

JVR: ...as it turns out now, 15 years later...

EVB: Now you tell me!

JVR: There weren't any other people in our school who were both doing stuff with computers as well as designing type. We naturally met during the course of our studies. And then there was a summer project where a whole bunch of us, students, got exploited into doing an extreme amount of work, for some exhibition that we hardly got paid for. And actually, we had a lot of fun during that program—that must have been '87 or '88—and we actually convinced the organization [this was a very large exhibition in Amsterdam] to get Apple to sponsor a machine, which they actually did! So we got a Mac SE and a LaserWriter.

EVB: Almost all of the graphics for the exhibition were done on a LaserWriter. [laughs] All of the signs, too, all of the really big panels...

JVR: The real design was set in *Univers*, but *Univers* wasn't available for PostScript at the time, so we went for the next best thing and set everything in *Helvetica*...

EVB: Oh, who can tell the difference? Come on!

JVR: There was no choice! We really loathed *Helvetica* at the time, but there was no *Univers* available, that's how primitive it was. Basically, the two of us were the only people in the project who could use the computer—the actual graphic designers of the project were not working with computers yet, so we had to operate that machine and typeset all that text.

What was the exhibition?
EVB: "Holland as Design." It involved various scenarios of how Holland could be designed or improved upon in the next 50 years.

JVR: There were experimental and environmental projects, and so on. That was the summer, and for the first time, we worked fairly closely together.

EVB: And we worked together in Berlin.

JVR: Yes, for my last internship, I went to Berlin to Erik Spiekermann's at MetaDesign, and that turned out to be fun...

Were you there at the same time together?
JVR: Yes, I kept in touch with Erik and told him that Berlin was an exciting city and there was interesting work to do—Meta was a nice, small studio at the time—only six or seven people. I was working on the ITC *Officina* typeface, basically finishing that from sketches and earlier artwork, and adding weights. This project was going well, and then Spiekermann came to Holland for a lecture and met up with Erik, who showed him his portfolio, and it turned out there was plenty of work to do on the *Officina* project, so Erik also came to Berlin for a while. During those days, in a time we were supposed to have a life, but didn't, we were working on the computers of MetaDesign.

Have you decided to remain a small shop?
JVR: We have fantasized, "what would happen if we opened a proper studio?" [laughs] And each time we asked ourselves, we came up with the answer, "Naaahhh." And I think that answer might have saved us in the end. I don't know—I think if we had actually grown as a studio, I don't know if we would still be working together as we are now.

EVB: That has never really been an issue, to have a physical company, or to have a physical studio. I think maybe in a while, when our kids grow up, things might be different, but we're not in a hurry. And there are *so* many design agencies in The Hague that it's really like a pack of hungry wolves—you know, you open up your shop, you buy your computers, you get your employees, and you have to get 100,000 euros worth of work right off.

Is it true, that there are more typographers per square meter in the Netherlands than any other country?
EVB: Yes, that's a Spiekermann quote...

JVR: ...sounds like it. But for a while the Academy in The Hague, as well as the Academy in Arnhem, were very successful in getting students interested in type design — and actually getting some skill into them so they could do it. Martin Majoor and Fred Smeijers are in Arnhem. But for a long time there was just Gerard Unger as the "young" type designer of Holland. After him came our generation of designers.

EVB: The Academy in the Hague was very successful, too. There were maybe 10 or 15 people who managed to make type professionally, and find a place in the business. Now the education continues, and it is still a part of the school curriculum. For some reason it just works.

JVR: Well, it's working slightly less these days, within the normal course, because there have been budget cuts and students don't get as many classes in type design as they used to.

EVB: Oh it was so much better in those good old days!

What impact has Holland, and Haarlem and The Hague, had on your approach to design?
EVB: That's a little hard to answer because it's like asking the fish how the water is...

JVR: In The Hague, though, or even Holland in general, there was a very fertile climate. We were a fairly lucky generation. There were a few older people, for example, Erik's brother, and a whole bunch of other people, who had already finished school and were practicing type designers. Our teacher, Gerrit Noordzij, encouraged the current students to be in touch with the former students and exchange visions, ideas, or criticisms of each other's work. So there were some "get-togethers"... *laughs* It's such a specialized field, that any contact you can get with your peers is great.

But it also seems like a very close knit community of designers — geographically and socially.
JVR: Yes, it was very motivating for me especially, because I would see my peers doing interesting work. But without that type of community, there might have not been as much motivation to dive into this subject so deeply.

EVB: At the time I was in school, we had computers for our last two years of study, but for the first three years we didn't. This was when Macintosh was about to "happen". But before desktop publishing, we both dabbled in computers — I had built one for my kids, and Just was building a ZX81 kit. And the act of type design was very abstract — there were cameras and drawing and painting for producing type — and we knew people who actually sold a type design to an actual type foundry, and sometimes we would talk to them, and it was all very exciting...

JVR: ..."He has a type design published, whoa!" *laughs* "That's pretty cool!"

EVB: But there was no clear application for it — it's not like there were job openings for type designers. But the lucky break was in '88 – '89 when Fontographer started to become available and Mac LaserWriters were out: well, we knew what to do with them. We knew how to make type already. And of course we had to learn the new digital tools, but that was easily solved. I guess we had a bit of an advantage — a lot of people also had to figure out type design as well as figure out the tools. There were a lot of people from The Hague who had type designs within the first five years of desktop publishing.

How do you begin a new typeface? Does the programming come first or do you start with the typeface?
JVR: It's so different. In the case of the TCDC typeface, it began with sketching. We had a couple of sessions where we would try out different constructions. In other cases, where we

have more abstract ideas, sometimes programming is involved early on in the process.

JVR: To flesh out this idea we didn't really need to do much programming.

EVB: But it always helps. From the beginning we don't really have to write code, but we can sort of get an idea of the machine we will have to build, to get it working. And we can build the shapes and the forms as part of the whole plan. It's not that hard. We have to make the typeface first, and then ask, "How are we going to have to program it?" It's not that we can write a specification for a program and give it to the programmer and say, "This is what we need", because we don't know what we need. It's just like with any design; you start with something, you try a couple of ideas, you get a better idea of where it should go, you make one or two prototypes, and so on.

There is never a clear path, or order, but it branches out from one clear point?
EVB: Yes. Start with one step, move to alternatives, choose another step, and so on. The shape that the program gets and the shape that the font will get evolve together. And in the end, you have something that is totally integrated. The shapes don't make much sense without the software, and the software doesn't make any sense without the shapes. But I think that's a good way of doing things.

JVR: It depends. A long time ago we did an experimental project called "BitPull" where the idea was to do something with bitmap shapes, but also to have control of the individual pixel shapes. During one brainstorming session we worked out how to implement that idea, using font technology, by not putting letters into the font but by adding pixel rows and then combining these. And it turned out that we had to start programming right away to make this concept get anywhere near useful.

EVB: A lot of people may have ideas that are similar, but then they have to stop because they don't know how to solve it. And the whole branch of investigation is never taken because that first step can't be initiated.

BitPull fonts in action. When used with the BitPuller application, bitmap fonts can be made in an infinite number of shapes.

JVR: The advantage of being able to program is that it changes how you think, and you can imagine how to solve certain problems. Automatically, you get ideas that you can only solve by writing some code. If you think you don't need to program yourself, you can obviously imagine something, some behavior, and write a spec and give that to a programmer, but...

EVB: ...But, then you get exactly that—that is what professional programmers do. They can build that one thing and that is what it will be. If the design process is any good you're already five steps further when it's done. Sometimes it's the code that pushes the shapes and sometimes it's the shapes that push the code.

How do you judge a good typeface?
JVR: By looking at it!

O.K. *(laughs)* **Now, if you had to explain this to someone who isn't familiar with the principles of typography, what would you say are some of the characteristics that define a good typeface?**
EVB: I'd ask: Is it done consistently? Are decisions taken for each shape, consistently applied

to other shapes? Because the letters of a typeface are not islands — they all share characteristics. Is it done appropriately for the media or technology it is in?

JVR: Is a text typeface suitable for setting a large amount of text?

EVB: That is why I think it is very hard to judge type design separately from typography. Because you can have a really good type design and still apply it in the most inappropriate way. I think Erik Spiekermann has a quote, "There aren't any real bad typefaces, there are just typefaces that are really difficult to apply."

Do you have a maxim for type design?
EVB: For the first five years we said, "Is best really better?" — that's a good one.

JVR: Tobias Frere-Jones has one: "We make things suck less."

EVB: That's also a good one...

JVR: But basically, he was only describing how he felt about the work he was doing at the time.

EVB: It depends upon the job, of course — sometimes you get a job that is bad and you have to make it less bad, and there's nothing you can do about it...

JVR: The "Is best really better?" motto came from "best" in the sense of absolute technical perfection — is that always preferable to things that look less technically perfect? — separating the quality of the typeface from the quality of its production.

EVB: For centuries, the goal of typography and printing was one — to make the best type possible on paper. And that went through all kinds of hiccups and delays but, paper has improved, printing types have improved, methods of making printing types have improved, and presses are better. I think for the last several years we've achieved that perfection — we can output 5000 lines on an inch, the highest, best resolution of fonts possible. Now, it's all possible! So designers are going for rougher paper, or polymer plates to get some kind of printing edge into it. And the whole "dirty faces" thing from the early Nineties was just a reaction to that. Of course that too has gotten old.

JVR: At the time, it was a logical reaction to Adobe *Garamond*, which was new in the late Eighties. It was really well done — it's a really well drawn typeface, and it's spaced really well, but in many cases, it's also really dull.

What is your most popular typeface and how would you explain its success?
EVB: In number of sales, it must be *Justlefthand-Erikrighthand* or *Trixie*.

Why those particular fonts, do you think?
EVB: I think in the beginning they stood out because there weren't any informal or loose or rough typefaces like that. We made a whole series in a relatively short period of time. Later on, their popularity was due to people already being familiar with them. These days, you can open a magazine and there's bound to be *Justlefthand* or *Erikrighthand* in one of the ads, or one of the pages.

JVR: They became popular relatively quickly when they came out.

For a while you saw *Trixie* everywhere! The "X-Files" titles, on candy wrappers, taco ads...
JVR: With *Justlefthand-Erikrighthand* we thought, "Hey, this is a cool gadget, perhaps people will like it for a few months..."

It's interesting that such a personal typeface made from your own handwriting would be your most popular seller to a whole bunch of strangers...
JVR: All of these fonts are made relatively

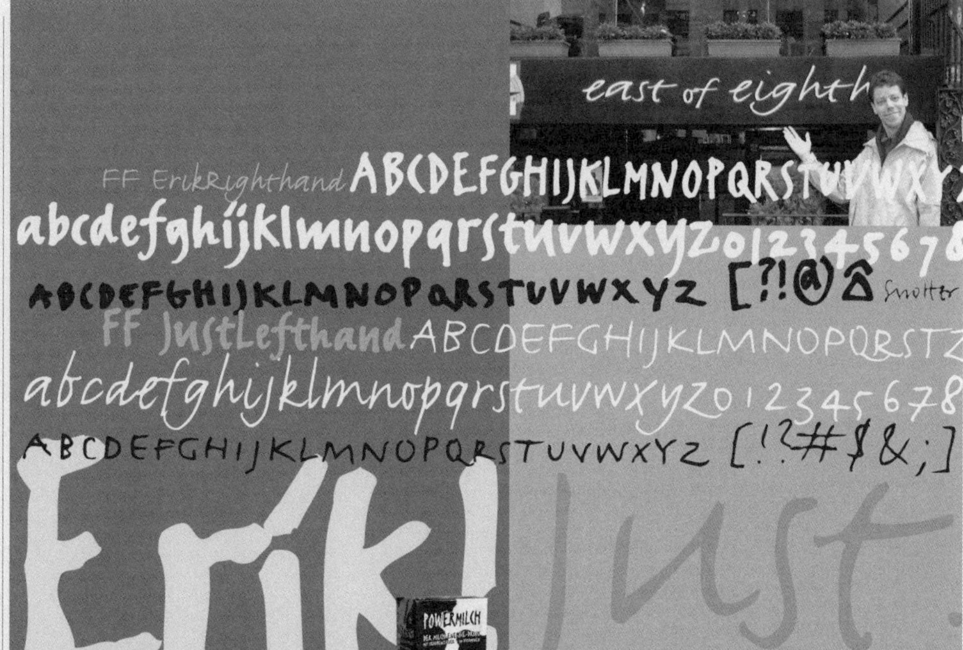

east of eighth
FF ErikRighthand ABCDEFGHIJKLMNOPQRSTUVWXY
abcdefghijklmnopqrstuvwxyz012345678
ABCDEFGHIJKLMNOPQRSTUVWXYZ [?!@] Snotter
FF JustLefthand ABCDEFGHIJKLMNOPQRSTZ
abcdefghijklmnopqrstuvwxyz012345678
ABCDEFGHIJKLMNOPQRSTUVWXYZ [!?#$&;]
Erik!
Just
POWERMILCH

FFKosmikA
bcdefghij
Hee!! daar gaat een Onomatopee! He
mmderdemmderdemm! en stiekem a
an zeeëgels denken en eidereendeiere
n zoeken, of aan sauerstoffflaschen
snuffelen en de Schifffahrt nog een
bekijken. TOEOEOET! Verdraaid, net t
e laat. TAATUU!! AAARGH!? IIIEEE!!
KLABAM!? Flippperende jazzzangeres
Anna wauwelt tegen Otto. Pffff! Daa
r gaat hij! Krokodil, snel er achter aa
n! WOEF! Ho stop mannetje! Jij bent e
rbij! "Verdrie" VRRROOOAAARRR! Ze zi
tten vlak achter ons! Harder, harder!
ergeant age
will have obs
he states ve
on Saturday
as a lovely m
o one o' cloc
ement to us w
she re-read
r she had pa

Specimens of LettError's *Justlefthand-Erikrighthand* (1990, top), *Kosmik* (1993, bottom left), and *Trixie* (1991, bottom right).

quickly. They are not extremely difficult to make from a type designer's perspective, but it happened that we were there at the right time once it became possible to make such typefaces — and with the right contact person — Erik Speikermann and FontShop. So we were there with Beowolf when FontShop started selling its own line of typefaces...

EVB: It was just plain luck...

JVR: Now you can find thousands of informal handwriting and dirty typewriter fonts online, free to download...

EVB: ...but people still use *Lefthand-Righthand* and *Trixie*...

JVR: They know these typefaces by name. They don't specify, "I want a dirty typewriter font" they say, "I want *Trixie*"...

Why should the public care about type design, or should they?

EVB: They shouldn't. For many, many applications, if the reader starts noticing the font or the typography, you've lost, because once readers start being aware of the type, they stop reading — and reading should be the goal.

JVR: From one standpoint, a good typeface should be totally unnoticeable. To an extent, we're going to try to do that with the most basic version of the Twin Cities typeface, but then again, it gets expanded in many different ways.

How can a typeface communicate what is special about a city (or can it) and what were some of the challenges you confronted when designing the Twin Cities font?

EVB: For the first presentation, this was basically the biggest problem we struggled with. The most obvious way, which is also the most horrible way to do it, would be to try to get some graphic element of the place into the shapes of the letters. So you get little high rises for a typeface about New York, or you get something metal with lattice work like the Eiffel Tower for a typeface about Paris, or double-decker buses for London, and it's just kitsch. To an extent our proposal is more about a city and diversity in general, rather than something specific from St. Paul and Minneapolis.

JVR: And this is even more important, because it is two cities.

EVB: So there's the element of diversity — I wanted something that became really flexible, and could be different things to different people, because that is what I think a city is. In that sense, it could be any city, but that should not make it less applicable for the Twin Cities. So that is where the concept came from — to build the pieces of a puzzle that could work together in many ways. I suppose you could find something historical typographically about a place, or ask someone who is from there. But I don't want to tell people what their city is about because, as I'm an outsider, they know more than me.

Perhaps once the font is unveiled, those kinds of interpretations are going to take shape naturally — connecting through usage.

EVB: Once we build the system, and the "typographic toy" [the online version of *Twin*, which automatically changes when it is linked to data on the Internet, such as weather, wind or personal parameters] is put out there and is publicly available, people will either like it or dislike it, but they hopefully will use it. I think that if it's available, it will become part of the city. People will start making notes with it, or pasting it up on their doors or windows, or maybe it will be used more publicly. It's a unique design — unique in that it's never been done before — although that is not necessarily a measure of quality. But if it gets around the city, it will become part of it, and then the situation is solved.

Were these ideas you were contemplating for your TCDC typeface something you had in the backs of your minds, or did they come out of the brief?

EVB: I had been puzzling over it for some time, without making any drawings or having any particular shapes in mind, but I think the concept can be extended beyond what we're doing now. It is a puzzle I find interesting from a type design point-of-view. The idea that one shape for one letter has some ideas of what the other shapes of other letters should be, but not all the way—if you draw a lower case 'e', you have some idea of what a lower case 'n' is going to look like, but not all of the decisions or the material you need to build the whole typeface are contained in this one letter. So for each letter you can build a number of alternatives—for example, for one 'n' you might make three or four 'e's' that go with it. And for each 'e' you can build another group of letters that might go with that.

The way that you would select those letters would be the same as the way a cook might select ingredients for a meal. If you start with 20 ingredients, and you need to cook a meal with five, you can make any number of flavors or dishes, just by picking the right ingredients in the right amounts.

So even though the shapes themselves don't change, just by picking particular variations of each letter, you can change the whole way the text is going to look. And of course this is really complicated to do, and no designer would ever follow any instructions we would write for that. But because we've already built a system that does typography, and does it interactively, and does it with computer code we can control, this is actually possible.

So users won't have to read manuals on how the letter combinations should form?

EVB: Right. Because then it would seem a bit contrived to go to all these lengths to come up with a particular set of letters, especially if you could just use another font. If the computer is doing it for you—and the computer can take a great number of things into account, and there are rules on how characters should combine, and any kind of interface that we decide to build for it—then, for example, there might be a Website with pretty straightforward typographic terms for manipulating the letters. But there could also be a parallel interface that says, "I want it rounder" or "I want it softer" or "it's my birthday". Or it could even tie bits of the typeface control into other values. For example, you can connect the typeface literally to what's going on in the city. It's one of the most exciting experiments because I really want to see if it's going to make sense. Can you tell a difference if you set a word at the beginning of the day vs. the end of the day? Can you see if something is going on, or does it just look like a random value? I think a typographic tool which responds to the city like that will be fun to have.

JVR: When we made *Beowolf*, we were wondering if it could respond to things, and now is the chance to try to do that.

Beowolf Beowolf
Beowolf Beowolf
Beowolf Beowolf
Beowolf Beowolf

Characters in LettError's first random typeface, *Beowolf* (1990). The more a particular letter is used, the more it degrades.

Beowolf **was a truly random program. Will the TCDC typeface have more planned randomness?**

EVB: The planned randomness is basically an idea you find in many of the other things we have done. As a designer I want to be able to control how something is going to look, but I also like the experience of being surprised. There are a great number of decisions in graphic design that are really totally arbitrary. For example, "is it red?" or "is it this typeface?" But there are also many issues that are not arbitrary, for example, "it has to be this big," "it has to be spaced this way". If you separate the things that *have* to be a particular way from the things that can vary and change, you can write a small program that makes a random choice. The trick is to find the right mix. We've built machines that come up with particularly graphic constructions or constellations of objects. You can look at them and say, "oh, this is crap, and so is this, and this one too, but hey, *this* is a really nice one," and the strange thing is that they are all built by the same rules — to the computer they're all identical. And it takes a human being to look at it and say "that is good" or "that is bad."

When we write computer code it's not that we're taking creative decisions out of the hands of the designer. We're just taking the dreary production stuff out of their hands and putting it into the hands of the computer, because the computer is much faster and more efficient at it. You still need a person to look at something and make aesthetic decisions to say, "well this is a really nice one, and the other 99 are bad."

Your TCDC proposal stated "...the user gets more control over issues previously left to the type designer... the designer gets more control over typography." Is there a connection between this idea of planned randomness and what you have just been discussing?

EVB: In a way. The typographer might like to say, "I want this glyph, and this glyph" but the system is going to say, "Well, actually, because this is the temperature, and this is the congestion in the city, or it's your birthday today, or whatever value we choose, you're going to have this one and this one instead."

Finally, what new LettError typeface can we look forward to in the future?

EVB: I want to make a series of more illustrative designs using our LetterSetter system, with more illustrated, colorful elements — not necessarily mice and varmints and cats and such. Somebody is also working on a toothpaste font — you know the shape of toothpaste you see in television commercials? It's called a "Nurdle". *laughs* If you do a "Google" search for it, you'll find a whole series of companies who build Nurdles. Anyway, we are making a toothpaste font...

Any last comments for your interview?

EVB: Well, perhaps it would be a good idea to say something about not being entirely sure about making a typeface for a city and that we hope that everybody in the city is going to like it, and if they don't, we're dreadfully sorry, but we tried!

The Glyph Model

We need a reference system for the type system. It's not difficult to spend hours drawing type, but in order to get a grip of the many variations some sort of direction is necessary.

In the sketch on the right there are 4 categories of parameters. At first we thought it was going to be two dimensional: an increase in one parameter would mean a decrease in another. Later it became clear that these parameters are not exclusive: it is possible to draw letters which fit in several groups at once. That means that each parameter can be seen as a dimension: the model can be drawn as a cube (far right)

The category names are quite subjective. The goal is not to classify the glyphs as belonging to one or the other, but to quantify each glyph.

Regular / Normal: the model needs some sort of plain reference point. Towards this point all glyphs become increasingly *normal*. Well, what we consider to be normal. No unusual forms or serifs, a sturdy low contrast sans serif design with subtle curves and rounded edges.

Formal / Serif: a slab serif sibling of the Regular / Normal sans. Towards this point all glyphs grow serifs.

Informal / Round: all shapes find curved alternatives. Rounder, more handdrawn sometimes cursive constructions.

Alternate / Weird: the place where all the scary creatures live. Strange and unusual alternatives.

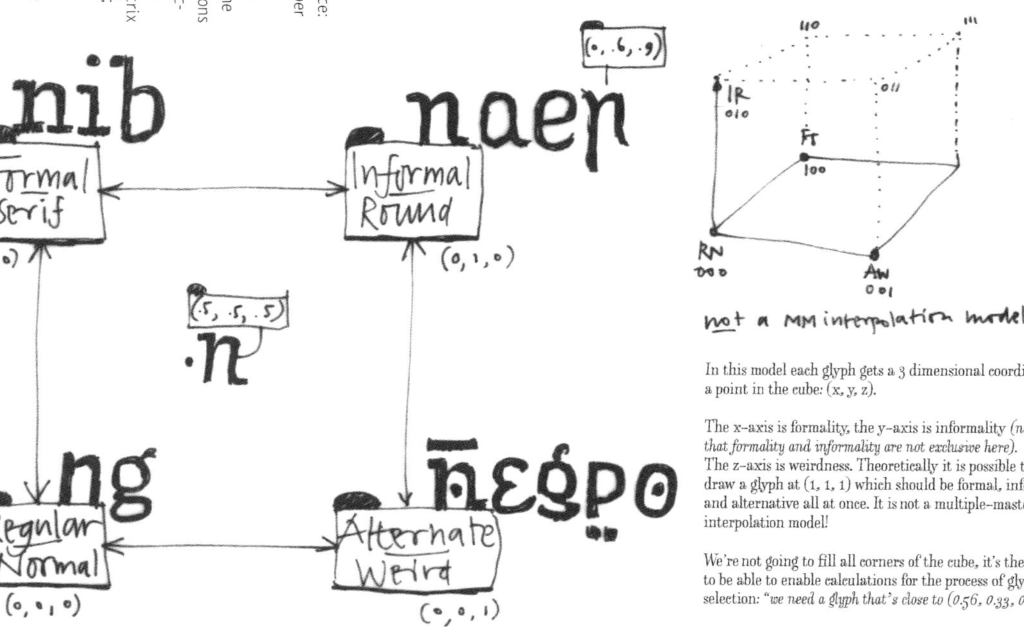

aving been awarded the "Typeface:
win Cities" commission in October
002, the first new step in the
ypeface design and development
rocess was for LettError to define
ne characteristics of the variations
n the letterforms for each charac-
er. Van Blokland and van Rossum
nitially proposed a quadratic matrix
ith four variations: formal/serif;
nformal/round; regular/normal;
nd alternate/weird. Later, the
egular/normal category would be
ropped because it was deemed
oo repetitive. January 2003.

In this model each glyph gets a 3 dimensional coordinate, a point in the cube: (x, y, z).

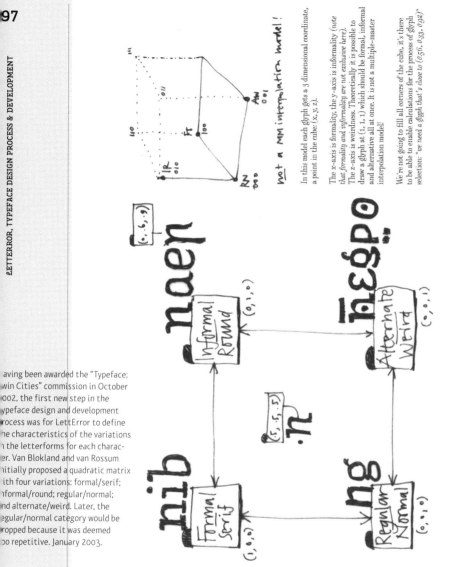

The x-axis is formality, the y-axis is informality *(note that formality and informality are not exclusive here)*. The z-axis is weirdness. Theoretically it is possible to draw a glyph at (1, 1, 1) which should be formal, informal and alternative all at once. It is not a multiple-master interpolation model!

We're not going to fill all corners of the cube, it's there to be able to enable calculations for the process of glyph selection: *"we need a glyph that's close to (0.56, 0.33, 0.92)"*

Twin City Design Celebration Type Design * January 24, 2003

A series of logotypes using glyph alternates to create different flavors in text The LetterSetter system is able to create any selection of glyphs and change the appearance of the text without clear transitions from one flavor to another.

Note that these are sketches, we intend to render the glyphs as smooth contours. But considering the smooth shapes take more time, this way we can quickly see which shapes are going to work and map the characterset before making an investment in precise drawings.

Missing in these samples are capitals, numbers, punctuation.

1.
Mainly Informal/Round

2
Mostly Formal/Serif

3.
Formal/Serif with some alternates.

4.
Regular/Normal with some alternates

5
Inbetween informal/round and alternate/weird.

6
Alternate/weird, almost a puzzle.

7
Regular/normal with some alternates.

8
Regular/normal with a conservative selection.

1 twin cities design celebration

2 twin cities design celebration

3 twin cities design celebration

4 twin cities design celebration

5 twin cities design celebration

6 twin cities design celebration

7 twin cities design celebration

8 twin cities design celebration

Initial logotype studies revealed the wide range of possibilities for setting "Twin Cities Design Celebration" in the *Twin* typeface. January 2003.

Once LettError set the matrix framework, they began the arduous task of filling in the rest of the characters for each descriptive sector. More samples of TCDC typemarks, including uppercase and lowercase, were tested to see how the letterforms would further mix together. January 2003.

LettError set variations of the logotype "Twin Cities Design Celebration 2003" using a computer program that would set random letters into the logotype. Some logos worked very well, while others did not, illustrating Erik van Blokland's point about the need to have a live person (rather than a computer) distinguish the "good" logos from the "bad" ones. March 2003.

ɪce enough characters
ɛre designed, further
ɔrd-setting tests showed
ɪw all ten typefaces in
e *Twin* family could
eate "flavors" in
ɔlock of dummy text.
ɔril 2003.

arms export trial Casual> Simon and the eplacements FormalRound> The Anne's Inn
BitRound> advermational BitRound> Serb union members questioned in spy satellite
tapes Loopy> The Ploughman and Horse Mixed> FionovetActivePowet Weird> THE
Mast and Book PosterSans> The Kettle and King Sans> British Prime Minister visits
stricken victims Casual> Turkish delegation cleared of murder coverup Weird>
THE PloughMan's Pub BitRound> German representatives questioned in refu-
gees tapes Formal> Republicans OK bomb bill. FormalWeird> KingsLey AND the Demo-
crats Sans> House Speaker opposes primitive bomb legislation. FormalRound> The William's Public House Sans> Communists BitRound> Alastair & the Republicans Max>
The Ploughman's Head Formal> German civil servants criticise export
subsidies legislation FormalRound> Croat representatives criticise phone
tap legislation Formal> Martin & the Madmen Max> Walters, Knox and Lawson
of Sunnyvale, CA Max> ForbesCarnegie Max> Serb official opposes encryption
bill Sans> Madmen Casual> infotainment Casual> Liz and the eplacements Weird> Lawyer
opposes gun control plan. Casual> The Prince's Head FormalWeird> Achim AND the Commitments PosterSans> The Irish's Head Weird> Dallas AND THE Commitments Formal> LWire Sans>
Caldecott M. Knox not to run for House Speaker. BitRound> Helen & the Things

Headlines, full paragraphs and various text sizes complete the concept development stage. April 2003.

TWIN CITIES DESIGN CELEBRATION 2003

Al's Toy Barn

REUTERS + + + Twin Cities Design Celebration. The string sketch from Monty Python's Instant Record Collection Transcribed from tape by Malcolm Dickinson CLARINET YALEVMX , 4/5/86. Adrian Wapcaplet: Aah, come in, come in, Mr....Simpson. Aaah, welcome to Mousebat, Follicle, Goosecreature, Ampersand, Spong, Wapcaplet, Looseliver, Vendetta and Prang! Mr. Simpson: Thank you. Wapcaplet: Do sit down--my name's Wapcaplet, Adrian Wapcaplet... Mr. Simpson: how'd'y'do. Wapcaplet: Now, Mr. Simpson... Simpson, Simpson... French, is it? S: Two thousand and three.

FoodStuff

American Airlines.

No. W: Aah. Now, I understand you want us to advertise your washing powder. S: String. W: String, washing powder, what's the difference. We can sell "anything". S: Good. Well I have this large quantity of string, a hundred and twenty-two thousand *miles* of it to be exact, which I inherited, and I thought if I advertised it-- W: Of course! A national campaign. Useful stuff, string, no trouble there. S: Ah, but there's a snag, you see. Due to bad planning, the hundred and twenty-two thousand miles is in three inch lengths. So it's not very useful. W: Well, that's our selling point! "SIMPSON'S INDIVIDUAL STRINGETTES!" S: What? W: "THE NOW STRING! READY CUT, EASY TO HANDLE, SIMPSON'S INDIVIDUAL EMPEROR STRINGETTES - JUST THE RIGHT LENGTH!" S: For what? W: "A MILLION HOUSEHOLD USES!" S: Such as? W: Uhmm...Tying up very small parcels, attatching notes to pigeons' legs, uh, destroying household pests... S: Destroying

FOOD * PHONE * GAS * DIESEL * LODGING

Type AND Typography•Fun AND Games

Downtowner

LURAY CAVERNS

The string sketch from Monty Python's Instant Record Collection Transcribed from tape by Malcolm Dickinson CLARINET YALEVMX , 4/5/86. Adrian Wapcaplet: Aah, come in, come in, Mr....Simpson. Aaah, welcome to Mousebat, Follicle, Goosecreature, Ampersand, Spong, Wapcaplet, Looseliver, Vendetta and Prang! Mr. Simpson: Thank you. Wapcaplet: Do sit down--my name's Wapcaplet, Adrian Wapcaplet... Mr. Simpson: how'd'y'do. Wapcaplet: Now, Mr. Simpson... Simpson, Simpson... French, is it? S: No. W: Aah. Now, I understand you want us to advertise your washing powder. S: String. W: String, washing powder, what's the difference. We can sell "anything". S: Good. Well I have this large quantity of string, a hundred and twenty-two thousand *miles* of it to be exact, which I inherited, and I thought if I advertised it-- W: Of course! A national campaign. Useful stuff, string, no trouble there. S: Ah, but there's a snag, you see. Due to bad planning, the hundred and twenty-two thousand miles is in three inch lengths. So it's not very useful. W: Well, that's our selling point! "SIMPSON'S INDIVIDUAL

MOTEL 6: first Left

HBO, Free Local Calls

STRINGETTES!" S: What? W: "THE NOW STRING! READY CUT, EASY TO HANDLE, SIMPSON'S INDIVIDUAL EMPEROR STRINGETTES - JUST THE RIGHT LENGTH!" S: For what? W: "A MILLION HOUSEHOLD USES!" S: Such as? W: Uhmm...Tying up very small parcels, attatching notes to pigeons' legs, uh, destroying household pests... S: Destroying household pests?! How? W: Well, if they're bigger than a mouse, you

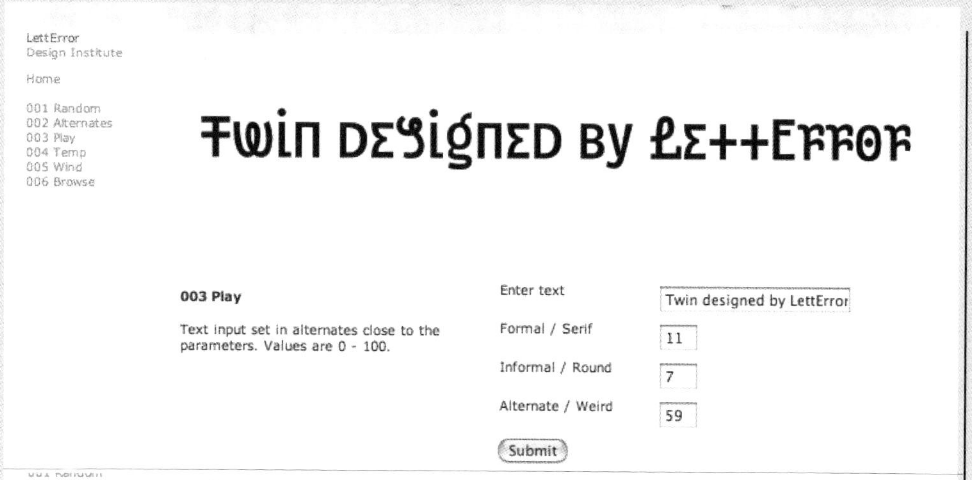

LettError
Design Institute

Home

001 Random
002 Alternates
003 Play
004 Temp
005 Wind
006 Browse

Twin designed by LettError

003 Play

Text input set in alternates close to the parameters. Values are 0 - 100.

Enter text	Twin designed by LettError
Formal / Serif	11
Informal / Round	7
Alternate / Weird	59

Submit

002 Alternates
003 Play
004 Temp
005 Wind
006 Browse

CAN A TYPEFACE REPRESENT A CITY?

003 Play

Text input set in alternates close to the parameters. Values are 0 - 100.

Enter text	CAN A TYPEFACE REPRESEN
Formal / Serif	50
Informal / Round	

ne online version of *Twin* can
ange on-the-fly in response to
namic data from the Twin Cities,
ch as wind and temperature, drawn
om the National Weather Service
recast Office, via the Web (see
terface 004, Temperature, below).
ttError has also created another
her interface (003 Play, top and
iddle) that allows the user to enter
lues of their own choosing, which
fect Twin's key axes of variability
ormal/Serif, Informal/Round,
ternate/Weird), producing remark-
le differences in the same text
nen entered in upper- and lowercase,
y, versus all caps. Interfaces 001
d 002, Random and Alternates,
rve up a random selection of
phabet glyphs, and an array of
fferent glyphs for the same
tter, respectively.

ages 104–105): Map of the Twin
ties family of typefaces.
2003 LettError Type & Typography.

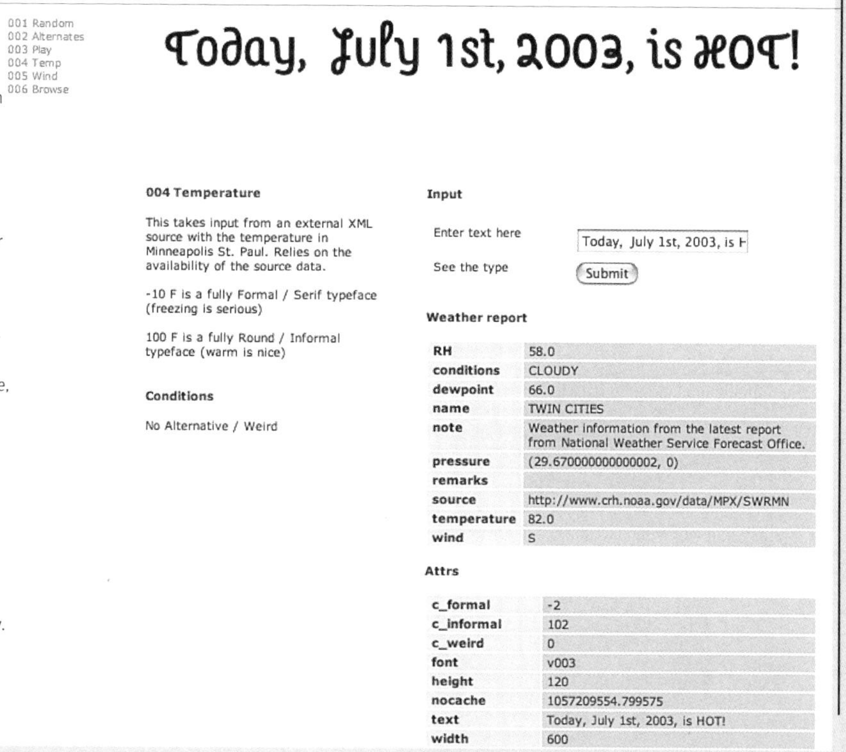

001 Random
002 Alternates
003 Play
004 Temp
005 Wind
006 Browse

Today, July 1st, 2003, is HOT!

004 Temperature

This takes input from an external XML source with the temperature in Minneapolis St. Paul. Relies on the availability of the source data.

-10 F is a fully Formal / Serif typeface (freezing is serious)

100 F is a fully Round / Informal typeface (warm is nice)

Conditions

No Alternative / Weird

Input

Enter text here	Today, July 1st, 2003, is H
See the type	Submit

Weather report

RH	58.0
conditions	CLOUDY
dewpoint	66.0
name	TWIN CITIES
note	Weather information from the latest report from National Weather Service Forecast Office.
pressure	(29.670000000000002, 0)
remarks	
source	http://www.crh.noaa.gov/data/MPX/SWRMN
temperature	82.0
wind	S

Attrs

c_formal	-2
c_informal	102
c_weird	0
font	v003
height	120
nocache	1057209554.799575
text	Today, July 1st, 2003, is HOT!
width	600

LETTERROR.COM 2003

MAP OF THE TWIN CITIES TYPEFACES

Obviously this is not a map of the twin cities themselves, but a specimen of the typeface disguised as a map.

The Twin Cities typeface can be many different things to different people. It consists of one very large character set with up to ten or fifteen alternate drawings for each letter. Also a database which tracks characteristics of each and an interactive, online system which blends and remixes the letters on request. The three main dimensions of the typeface are named Serif/Formal, Round/Informal and Alternate/Weird. All axes start in an arbitrary center of design space, we choose the Sans it has lots of room to sprout serifs and whatnot. Different combinations of these dimensions show specific areas with distinct flavors and characteristics. The LetterSetter (online) version of Twin Cities does it all. This specimen is an overview of a set of fonts, neighborhoods if you like, which we handpicked from the large collection of shapes. A short introduction of each of the fonts follows. ✦

SANS #1

An arbitrary center to the city. It could have been any of the other designs. For the interactive version, the Alternator, there's no difference. Twin Cities Sans is a nice and simple typeface with short ascenders and descenders. And a very low cap-height. It's kind of narrow and not entirely straight.

FORMAL #2

At first sight, the FORMAL avenue just grows serifs when it travels further from the SANS. But step by step each letter transforms into a more grown up version of itself. Older and perhaps more conservative make their appearance. It becomes a sturdy slab serif typeface, Posh & Classy. Parks and avenues with museums and concert halls.

ROUND #3

Obviously SANS & FORMAL assume that they're the only place in town where one would like to reside. Fortunately, there is more to choose from. There are places which do not follow grand plans and imposing architecture. Places which have a more organic texture, a more human approach to things. Maybe not everything is as clean and tidy, but it can be welcome contrast to the harsh atmosphere of the city.

WEIRD #4

By definition, any kind of structure leaves a certain number of elements as unclassifiable. Things that don't fit in any box or category. Quickly souls like

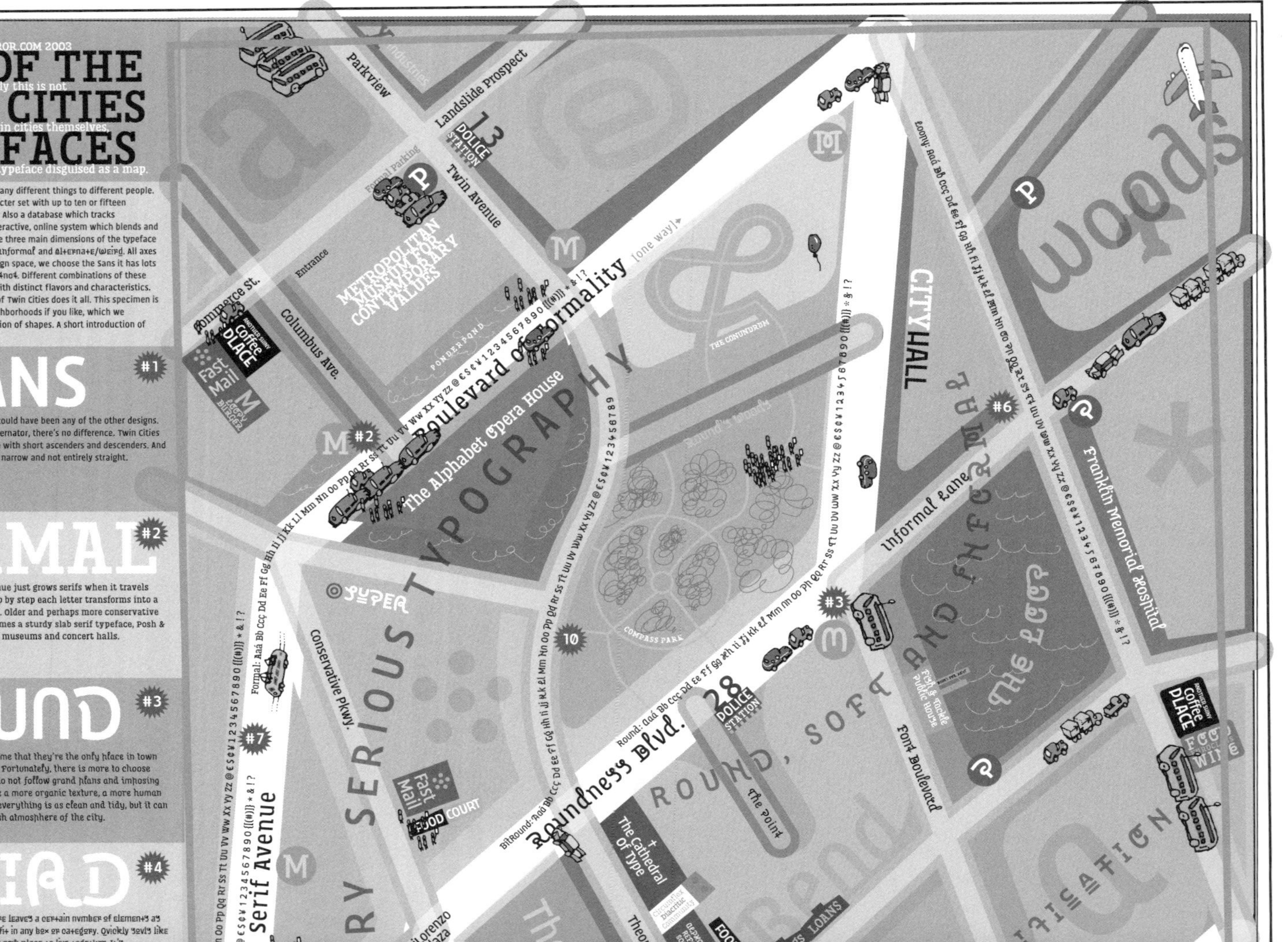

Rooted in typefaces designed (sometimes painted) specifically for advertising posters. Type in the city consists for a substantial part of advertising: brand names, logos and billboards. Walker Evans documented urban typography in the nineteen thirties and it remains a source of inspiration today. PosterSans is a fine blend of shapes from the Alternator© catalog. * INSTANT LOGOS! * Deli@ious Pizza! * Fast Food! * It Exterminates RATS! * It washes DISHES * It takes out STAINS!

Loony #6

Each letter shows its looniest and roundest alternative. As if it was spring and all letters decided to sprout little typographic tendrils, reaching out across the word. Perhaps a hopeless case for the corporate world of Sans & Formal. Loony is a romantic, unexpected small park, just around the corner, never noticed but centuries old. Strange, you never saw it before, you make a point to remember and come back next week and take the kids.

Casual #7

Casual is that strange transition between Sans and Formal. A complex list of opposing criteria: open, but not too open. Friendly, but not forward. Strict, but not imposing. What? It's got serifs, but not too many. Just a few of the letters have grown them, others are still thinking about it. In transition from one state to the other.

W.Round #8

On the corner of Weird and Round. It's round, there's no doubt about that. But the letters have grown funkier than the Round and Loony varieties. Why not? The Alternator has opened the roads to this part of town and we might as well take a quick look around. Yes, it is a strange duck (as we say) but nothing to apologize for. Strange is not bad, it just takes some time to get to know the area. First impression: safe&OK.

Gothic #9

Before Sans knew what it was, it was Gothic. Though Sans seems to have forgotten it's roots, Gothic makes an effort every now and them to remind them. It's Sans, but then a couple blocks south, towards Weird/Alternate. Letters that aren't regularized and straightened out. Not as flashy as it's cousin PosterSans either. Gothic has an impressive lineage, but it won't tell, so you just have to bike over there and take a look yourself. It's not so far.

BitRound 10

When you take the Avenue between Round and Sans, you can stop in the middle and take a look at BitRound. Not as hard, not as round. Somewhere in between.

©&®

Twin Sans

ABCDEFGHIJ

KLMNOPQR

STUVWXYZ

abcdefghi

jklmnopqr

stuvwxyz

0123456789

{(!?&$⊗£@*:;,.)}

¶

Twin Formal

A B C D E F G H I J

K L M N O P Q R

S T U V W X Y Z

a b c d e f g h i

j k l m n o p q r

s t u v w x y z

0 1 2 3 4 5 6 7 8 9

{ (! ? & $ ⊗ £ @ * : ; , .) }

¶

Twin Round

ABCDEFGHIJ

KLMNOPQR

STUVWXYZ

abcdefghi

jklmnopqr

stuvwxyz

0123456789

{(!?&$¤£@⁘:;,.)}

¶

A B C D E F G H I J

K L M N O P Q R

S T U V W X Y Z

a b c d e f g h i

j k l m n o p q r

s t u v w x y z

0 1 2 3 4 5 6 7 8 9

{ (! ? & $ % £ @ * : ; , .) }

¶

Twin Poster Sans

A B C D E F G H I J

K L M N O P Q R

S T U V W X Y Z

a b c d e f g h i

j k l m n o p q r

s t u v w x y z

0 1 2 3 4 5 6 7 8 9

{ (! ? AND $ ✖ £ AT * : ; , .) }

¶

A B C D E F G H I J

K L M N O P Q R

S T U V W X Y Z

a b c d e f g h i

j k l m n o p q r

s t u v w x y z

0 1 2 3 4 5 6 7 8 9

{ (! ? & $ ¤ £ @ ⁘ : ; , .) }

Twin Casual

ABCDEFGHIJ

KLMNOPQR

STUVWXYZ

abcdefghi

jklmnopqr

stuvwxyz

0123456789

{(!?&$⊗£@*:;,.)}

¶

Twin Weird Round

ABCDEFGHIJ

KLMNOPQR

STUVWXYZ

abcdefghi

jklmnopqr

stuvwxyz

0123456789

{(!?&$€£@*:;,.)}

¶

Twin Gothic

ABCDEFGHIJ

KLMNOPQR

STUVWXYZ

abcdefghi

jklmnopqr

stuvwxyz

0123456789

{(!?&$⊗£@*:;,.)}

Twin BitRound

ABCDEFGHIJ

KLMNOPQR

STUVWXYZ

abcdefghi

jklmnopqr

stuvwxyz

0123456789

{(!?&$⊗£@⁘:;,.)}

¶

TYPE FOR THE TWINS: A REVIEW OF THE TCDC PROPOSALS

Michael Worthington

FOUNDATIONS

When we learn to read, we are taught to view the written word as a concept rather than a form. The result is that most readers bypass how the message looks (the typeface) and head straight for the meaning of the words, which is the main purpose of written language after all. Do readers ever pay attention to typefaces? Typographers and type designers do, and I would guess some graphic designers, too. These typophiles believe the reader is somehow affected by the designer's choice of one typeface over another; they have faith in the importance of what they do; they presume their professions make a difference in the world.

Being on the side of the typophiles, I would argue that everyone is affected by typographic form, but primarily on a subconscious level. Those malleable letter shapes provide a context for the word's meaning, by suggesting a certain time-period, having a certain attitude, or even stirring an emotion in the reader. The type becomes adjective: it can look bookish or frivolous, authoritarian or joking; italic type can look fast, icy type cold, shattered type dangerous. If the word says "house" you think of an image of a house in your head, and depending on what typeface the word is set in the house can be old and stately, mid-century modern, futuristic, cozy, haunted etc. What the word directly describes is the primary signifier (e.g. the house); what the form indirectly suggests is the secondary signifier (e.g. what kind of house it is). No matter how little attention we pay to those secondary signifiers, they are quietly working behind the scenes, subconsciously affecting our reading of the primary meaning.

a | a | a | *a* | a

. The letter 'a' set in (left to right): elvetica Roman, Times Roman, Futura Book, cotch Roman Italic, and Lubalin Graph.

Typography functions as a consensual visual language; each letter in the alphabet has a set of core skeletal shapes which everyone agrees makes that particular letter recognizable and distinguishable from other letters. For example, a lowercase 'a' can be set in *Helvetica Roman*, *Times Roman*, *Futura Book*, *Scotch Roman Italic*, or *Lubalin Graph* (FIGURE 1). The type designer dresses up these basic skeletons of the alphabet in order to convey meaning. This process is a delicate one, the palette of shapes is limited, and you can't be too pictorial since the letters still have to be read as letters. It takes considerable skill to subtly suggest associations in the reader's mind using only the blunt instrument of type design. Understanding and controlling a typeface's capacity for communication is at the heart of the TCDC identity.

How can the complexities and individual traits of a city be represented with such a crude and subjective vehicle as typography? The task of understanding and representing the distinctive character of any city (let alone two!) is a daunting one. Reaching consensus on the essential experience of the Twin Cities is unlikely due to their social, generational, economic and ethnic diversity; each sub-population experiences its own version of the city, effectively a different city. In the proposals for the TCDC identity, three strategies for creating a pertinent connection between type design and the Twin Cities seem to emerge: to invest a typeface with a variety of qualities (multiple secondary signifiers) in order to parallel the city's social structure; to use an aspect of architecture as a metaphor for creating a typeface; or to embrace the subconscious and subjective nature of meaning inherent in type design, and make a typeface that connotes adjectives obliquely descriptive of the Twin Cities.

BLUEPRINTS

Type design is rarely used as the means of creating citywide identity. The visibility and permanence of architecture makes it a more obvious choice: Paris and the Eiffel Tower, Sydney and the Opera House, the Guggenheim in Bilbao, Big Ben, the Empire State Building, the Statue of Liberty, the Golden Gate Bridge. Such architecture becomes graphic icon, reappearing on t-shirts, buttons, baseball caps and coffee mugs for a 10-mile radius around each monument. One of the few cities with a distinct typographic icon is Hollywood, California, where the monument itself (the Hollywood sign) is made of type, though the neon signage of Las Vegas might arguably make it the only city recognizable through its typographic landscape. There are certainly national stereotypes in type design (acknowledging the sweeping nature of stereotypes): the designs of typographer Roger Excoffon (*Antique Olive*, *Mistral*, *Banco*) could be seen as typically French, flamboyant, liberated and idiosyncratic; the hefty types of the American Ozwald Cooper, by contrast, are overweight and shout loudly across the page; the precise and neutral designs of Max Miedinger's *Swiss Helveti(c)a* are another stereotype (FIGURE 2). National traits in type design were once formed by the typographic history and legacy of the country and culture where type designers were educated or practiced—could *Gill Sans*' classical form of modernity really come from anywhere other than innately cautious and xenophobic England?—though this

Ooooh la la!
Antique Olive

The City of Lights.
Mistral

MERCI BEAUCOUP.
BANCO

Ketchup & Freedom fries!
Cooper Black Italic

Pardon me, do you have the time?
Helvetica

2. Character samples from *Antique Olive*, *Mistral*, *Banco*, *Cooper Black*, and *Helvetica*.

has diminished somewhat with the rapid global exchange of local design ideas and forms.

Many major institutions that represent cities—from sports teams to museums—have used distinctive typography to express their core values and to gain a unique identity. The typography for a sports team usually relies heavily on crude secondary signifiers. The shape of the type aligns closely with the desired attributes of the team, usually aggressive, fast and physically foreboding—that Timberwolves type sure looks fierce! The typographic identities for certain arts institutions have used subtler signifiers and strategies of implementation to express their more esoteric virtues and values. One enduring example is in Minneapolis itself: Matthew Carter's modular type design for the Walker Art Center. Carter created a typographic frame with five different kinds of "snap-on" serifs. Intended to reflect the Walker's "multi-voiced" mission, the identity also expresses the energy and contemporary nature of the Walker (FIGURE 3). Another example is Bruce Mau's identity for the Netherlands Architecture Institute (NAi), which used only one logotype but projected it onto 100 surfaces and then rendered it in 1,000 different colors, to create a dialogue between space, light and texture, appropriate to the concerns of an architecture organization (FIGURE 4). The Tate Modern in London has a similarly fluid identity designed by Wolff Olins, where a nebulous logo has optional amounts of blur applied to it in order to keep it in flux (FIGURE 5). Projects such as these imply that fixed meaning is out of fashion, suggesting instead fluidity, (the illusion of) choice, and that evolving identities have greater longevity and can communicate to a more diverse audience.

One of the few successful examples of a city commissioning a typeface (as opposed to a logo) for its identity is Glasgow in Scotland. Honored as the UK City of Architecture and Design in 1999, Glasgow held a competition to design a corporate typeface, with participants such as Jonathan Barnbrook, Jeremy Tankard and The Foundry. The winner was Erik Spiekermann's design studio MetaDesign, whose concept involved a font with different ligatures for different pronunciations of the same letter combinations, reflecting the vocal tones particular to the Glasgow region (FIGURE 6). Though the end result was a simplified version, Meta's solution succeeded on many fronts. The typeface formally related to the city's industrial heritage—grid-like, heavy, tough and rough—but also included a decorative historical nod to Glasgow's most visible architect and designer Charles Rennie Mackintosh. The

WALKER ART CENTER

WALKER ART CENTER

WALKER ART CENTER

WALKER ART CENTER

3. Four settings of the Walker Art Center's custom typeface, *Walker* (1995), employing variations of "snap on" serifs applied to the letterforms. Designed by Matthew Carter. Image courtesy of the Walker Art Center.

4. In 1993, Bruce Mau developed an elastic logotype for the Netherlands Architecture Institute (NAi) that would allow the local and in-house designers maximum freedom for interpretation and experimentation. Image courtesy of Bruce Mau Design, Inc.

TATE TATE

TATE TATE

. Wolff Olins created a distinctive rand for the Tate Modern in London: the ord "Tate" is modeled to provide a range f logos that appear to be in and out of ocus. These are used freely, suggesting ne dynamic nature of Tate's point of iew. Image courtesy of Wolff Olins.

. After winning the commission to esign a typeface for the *UK City of rchitecture and Design* festival, letaDesign created *Glasgow* (1999). nspired by the vocal pronunciations articular to the Glasgow region. nage courtesy of Erik Spiekermann.

Glasgow is
Scottish in its stone,
European
in its urban pedigree,
and American
in its gridiron plan.

type reflected the language of the local population by attempting to replicate distinctive colloquial pronunciation through typographic expression. The final version contained a series of variable characters, ligatures and underscores that could be inserted at will by the designer, allowing for flexibility and a sense of ownership.

Historically, typefaces have been shaped by the possibilities and limitations of the technology used to produce them. In part, Gutenberg's type looked a certain way because of the tools used to make the letters and to print the pages. The same can be said of metal type, photosetting, and the bitmap and "experimental" typefaces produced with digital drawing tools in the late Eighties and early Nineties. During this period certain type designers purposefully broke the traditional rules of "good" typography and examined the borders of legibility and readability (see Neville Brody's *FUSE*, or early issues of *Emigre* [FIGURE 7]). Such experiments destabilized the historically conservative, established type foundries and gave graphic designers cultural permission to become type designers. Though many typefaces of this period were cul-de-sacs in terms of functionality, they were necessary to dramatically shift the trajectory of the world of type design. Prior to this moment, typeface design had involved immense labor and expense, and was inaccessible to most type-design-wannabes. The first forays into type design for "Typeface: Twin Cities" competition participants such as Conor Mangat and LettError were early Macintosh-based experiments. The Mac also formed the basis of type design practice for others such as Sibylle Hagmann and Eric Olson.

From this rebellious genesis a second wave of type design, which carefully examined aspects of the history of typography, occurred throughout the mid 1990s and early 2000s. The resulting typefaces were less overtly experimental, their designers opting instead to pay more attention to craft (e.g. Zuzana Licko's *Mrs. Eaves*, Jens Gehlhaar's *CIA Compendium*, Jonathan Hoefler's *Knockout* or *Proteus Project* [FIGURE 8]). The quirks are quieter and technological developments are a core component in the way the typeface is used: modular characters, interchangeable weights, MultipleMasters, intelligent ligatures, random fonts and "smart" fonts linked to databases, are some of the possibilities that have been explored. The technology is used to liberate either typographer or designer from his or her traditional role of producing single fixed solutions to a typographic problem. This kind of systematic use of technology is clearly reflected in the TCDC proposals by Peter Biľak,

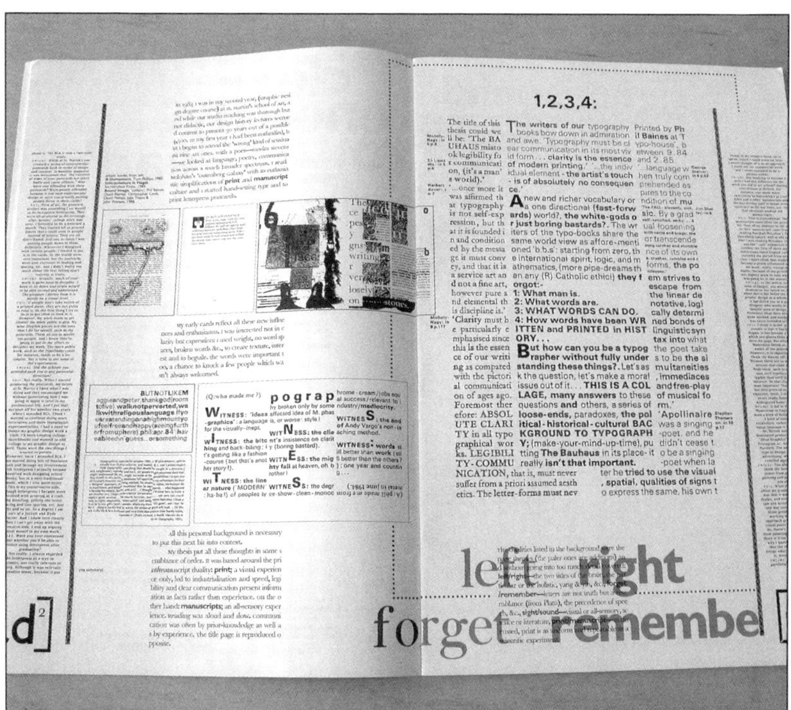

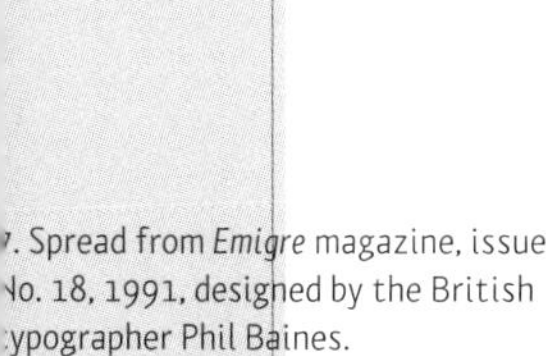

7. Spread from *Emigre* magazine, issue No. 18, 1991, designed by the British typographer Phil Baines.

8. Type specimens from Zuzana Licko's *Mrs. Eaves* (1996), Jens Gehlhaar's *CIA Compendium* (1998), and Jonathan Hoefler's *Proteus Project* (1996).

Mrs. Eaves Small Caps

FANCY

MRS. EAVES ITALIC

SMOOTH

Mrs. Eaves Bold

cheeky

Mrs. Eaves Italic

sparkly

CIA Antigill

CIA

CIA Earthworm

CIA

CIA Humdrum

CIA

CIA Dogsear

CIA

Ziggurat

Ss *Ss*

Leviathan

Ss *Ss*

Saracen

Ss *Ss*

Acropolis

Ss *Ss*

Sibylle Hagmann and especially LettError, all of whom use some kind of modular element to mirror the constantly evolving nature of the city.

The six type designers and design studios who accepted the University of Minnesota Design Institute's invitation to submit proposals provide a breadth of solutions, proving that typography can be a rich and fertile ground for growing metaphors, as well as clarity, branding and conceptual strategy. The results highlight how the once "invisible" art of type design is evolving into a practice with sophisticated concepts and intelligent use of contemporary technology—maintaining its relevance as a means of communication in contemporary culture.

The typefaces produced for this competition are conceptual solutions conveyed through the form of the type and the implementation of typographic systems and rules. While the importance of well-crafted letters was recognized by the entrants, form grew from appropriate concepts, resulting in solutions that are pragmatic and poetic, emotive and functional. If the typeface is the city, these cities have well kept roads and clean streets, but plenty of character too; they are cities where intelligence, beauty, originality and individuality are all appreciated.

◎◎◎◎

CONSTRUCTIONS AND FABRICATIONS

There are two men at my door, dressed in dark gray and looking serious. On the left is a tall thin gentleman, gaunt with even features; the man on the right is carrying encyclopedias. They ask me questions, try to sell me something. I have a funny feeling they want to teach me something. I'm in my pajamas and the brisk morning air is turning my feet purple. I glance at my toes and when I look back up at the men their appearance seems to have changed. The tall skinny man now appears shorter than I remembered, and broader too. He's definitely the same man, but his appearance has shifted. The man on the right seems to be dressed in different clothes now. He still holds the encyclopedias, but his suit is lighter, and the cut sharper. I close the door before they can finish speaking to me and I think to myself, "It's going to be a very strange day".

Peter Biľak's initial solution for the TCDC identity was to create a metamorphosing typeface, one that transforms and adapts to its surroundings, a reflection of the mutable nature of cities and their occupants.

The typeface uses an aspect of OpenType technology—specifically a feature intended for instances where the justification of Arabic text is required—which allows the software to control the width of each character by making a selection from a range of glyphs. When the text block setting is justified, the software selects the glyph with the appropriate width as opposed to stretching the characters. The character spacing remains the same (unlike traditional digital justification methods where the character width remains fixed and the spacing expands or contracts) creating an evenness and visual harmony between blocks of text whether the line length is comparatively long or short (SEE P. 38).

Bilˇak creatively subverts the technology, cleverly using it for a purpose for which it wasn't intended, but the technology gets revenge by dictating the designer's formal choices. Bilˇak is steered toward designing a light monoline sans serif, since these letterforms are more readily interchangeable and are sympathetic to being condensed or expanded while retaining a consistent tone. The end result is that the letterforms feel overly reductive (formally and connotatively), and are overshadowed by the novel use of technology.

By his own admission Bilˇak ended up "solely representing the possibilities of OpenType [and] ignoring the original assignment" and this realization led him to submit a second proposal. Here Bilˇak's primary objective clearly relates to the brief: to raise the public's awareness of typography, and use the TCDC identity as a tool to educate the public about the history of type design. Bilˇak proposed a system whereby a single font, *History*, would appear in the font menu of the designer's computer and would access a local database and a substantial type library (SEE P. 40). Depending on the day, a different typeface would automatically be chosen from the library; each typeface would be part of a chronology of type design from Gutenberg's invention of moveable type, through to the latest typeface of 2003. Beneath the TCDC 2003 logo a smaller piece of text would name the typeface, its designer and date of creation, giving the public a potted history of type design. This facile notion builds a comprehensive platform for typographic education, and although the practicalities of implementation remain unresolved, it is one of the most compelling proposals presented. A notable aspect of the proposal is that the conceptual solution precludes the type designer from making any new form; resolution is reached by way of curating and strategy rather than form-making. Bilˇak explains, "I am genuinely interested in exploring this notion of design, not just the physical production... the Twin Cities project was my attempt 'not to design anything.'" Bilak's solution appears to refute the power of form; he claims the solution is "not about formal or aesthetic solutions." Conversely, the solution is entirely about the form and aesthetics of type design—those in the historical canon rather than those being invented for this project.

◎◎◎◎

I leave the house to walk down the street to the grocery store. I need bread and milk. Don't get distracted by the special offers. Don't forget the essentials. The street seems strange, its angles harsher than usual, more uniform. I find myself more aware of the architecture than I ever have been, and while I'm gazing up at the buildings I walk smack into a lady pushing a baby stroller. My force knocks the stroller over and the two babies inside roll across the pavement. I rush to pick them up before they can come to any harm. The first child is skinny and energetic, screaming and throwing her arms around wildly. The second child is rotund, stronger and heavier than her sibling, yet stoic and silent. I tuck one under each arm and return them to the stroller. They seem happier now that they are all back together. It's only now that I notice their mother, elegant and composed, a woman whose unconventional beauty steals my breath for a second.

The starting point for Sibylle Hagmann's font was historical and contemporary photographs of the Twin Cities. Taking the architectural shapes and perspective lines as the basis for a grid, she created letter shapes that reference the urban space of the two cities. From this methodical and mathematical starting point Hagmann set about building a foundation of maximum readability. With these guidelines in place less regimented experimentation was allowed, creating a more idiosyncratic and eclectic set of letters while keeping enough common features to retain harmony. This mix of strict rules and unfettered experimentation is common in Hagmann's work and reflects the contrasting ideologies of her education at the Basel School of Design in Switzerland and at California Institute of the Arts in Valencia, California.

Hagmann's *Twin Cities* is a typeface full of oddities. The cuts used to create the illusion of thicks and thins give the type a humanist feel despite its mechanistic tendencies. The modular construction of the letterforms is tempered by asymmetric cross-strokes ('f' and 't'), slightly curved finials ('a', 'd', 'r' and 'u'), and irregular slab serifs in the capitals. These, and other arbitrary quirks make the individual letterforms original and inventive (look at the foot of the '9' and the stem extended above the apex of the '4' [SEE P. 74]). Indeed, Hagmann's typeface has so many irregularities that the characters shouldn't really fit together into a coherent alphabet, but they do. In what is essentially a text face, the only characters that seem to break the rhythm are the 'm', 'n' and 'w', which ironically stand out because they adhere too strictly to the 45 and 90 degree grid, creating character shapes traditionally associated with upper case letters; they appear to be wider than their companions (SEE P. 72).

Hagmann used the framework of her Twin Cities font to create two sympathetic typefaces that reflect the formal differences in architecture between St. Paul and Minneapolis. The resulting display typefaces—*St. Paul Thin Script* and *Minneapolis Super Bold*—have much louder secondary signifiers and more decorative forms than the more functional *Twin Cities*. Together they combine with a set of abstract elements based on perspective lines and architectural features to give the designer a palette of forms from which to compose potential logos for TCDC 2003 (SEE P. 73 & 75). There is no single authoritarian solution as is commonplace in traditional identity design (the fixed logotype). Instead the system acknowledges the complexity of the city and its ever-changing nature, and reflects this in a mutable logo that offers a multitude of possible solutions.

◎◎◎◎

He's working on the construction site again. I see him every day when I go out for my daily walk; he always wears the same clothes, simple black jeans and a long-sleeved black shirt. He's tall and well built, a strong man with plenty of muscle. He's working hard bending rods of metal into perfectly-shaped loops. He takes his job seriously, you can tell, the pride is clear. He looks like he's worked on the construction site for all his life, and that he'd be happy to stay there too. I wave to him, and he waves back. As he turns around to bend more metal I notice a copy of Italo Calvino's INVISIBLE CITIES in his back pocket.

Eric Olson began his process with an architectural idea: by building a typographic skeleton that could serve as the foundation for more complex levels of growth, he could echo the expansion of the Twin Cities from their humble beginnings as trading river cities. The two companion typefaces—one neutral and honest, the other more elaborate and expressive—also reflect what Olson saw as polar opposites co-existing in the Twin Cities: liberal yet conservative; progressive yet historically proud; the Walker Art Center yet the Mall of America.

TCDC Sans serves its purpose as a solid but familiar basis for the friendly and accessible *TCDC Display*, the second, and more noteworthy of the two typefaces (SEE P. 28). There are curves where uprights and horizontal strokes meet, and the characters are very full—the 'G' and 'O' nearly circular—giving the impression of a slightly expanded typeface. The rounded apex and vertex of the 'M', 'W' and 'N' break the consistent cap height, making the type feel lively and informal, and this is further enforced by the irregular arms of the 'E', 'S' and 'C' (though the 'C' ultimately feels unbalanced—a little too top heavy—as Olson tried to put some individual traits into one of the uppercase letters in the logotype TCDC [SEE P. 27]).

The typeface's congeniality is tempered by an industrial allusion—each letter feels like it was created from a single rod of iron, heated and bent into shape. The type is slightly awkward and overweight, yet these factors work in Olson's favor, preventing the typeface from being overly precious. The forms seem to reference Minneapolis's industrial heritage without directly quoting the vernacular, allowing the type to be both retro and contemporary. Olson's font reflects a perfect mix of geometric functionality and humanistic desire, a conflict he is intrinsically aware of: "I'm a traitor to the traditionalists because I'm too strict to fully embrace the influence of the pen yet I can never make a fully geometric face work well."

Olson went on to develop his *TCDC* proposal into a font called *Locator* consisting of six different weights, all with italics, and six capitals-only versions called *Locator Display*. Like many typefaces created for a specific purpose (e.g. *Times*, *Bell Centennial*, *Meta*) Olson's *Locator* (SEE P. 35) should find an audience far beyond its initial aspirations.

I buy what I need from the shops. I manage to stick to the basics as much as I can. Just what I need. The checkout clerk rings up the prices. As usual, it's more than I thought and I don't have enough money. At first she looks like the other checkout girls, but when I look at her face more closely, she's strange and pretty, her features all a little too large or too small. I think she's maybe from another country. She smiles and lets me off paying the few cents I don't have. As I leave the store I think to myself that I'd like to get to know her better, even though I know I'll never see her again.

Gilles Gavillet and David Rust, of Optimo, created a solution that stems from the city's urban planning and navigational systems; they utilize the symbolic language of maps and street signs and integrate them with letterforms to create a system reflecting "the urgent aesthetic that you meet in maps, plans or manuals."

The basic monoline typeforms that Optimo created are squarish, reminiscent of *Gridnik*, OCR-B or *Eurostile*, with some characteristics of a monospaced typewriter font thrown into the mix. These contradictions of referent allow the typeface to gain its own identity through a mixture of individual and unexpected traits in the lowercase letterforms. The tail of the 'g' is unnaturally short, creating little disruption to the baseline of the phrase "Twin Cities Design 2003"; the 't' is unusually wide in both its tail and its cross-stroke; the foot of the unconventional 'i' is as wide as the width of the 'w'; while the 'e' and the 's' gain their individual character from their arms, which extend and enclose the counterspace (SEE P. 64).

Optimo created a set of urban shapes to complement and combine with these letterforms (SEE P. 65). Inspiration came from an architecture magazine from the late Sixties featuring airport plans and signage; they were struck by one particular signage solution where every terminal number was placed in a geometrical shape so as to be immediately recognizable. The simplistic relationship between shape and letter appealed to Gavillet and Rust, and using simple forms they created a "play kit" for the designer where the font and symbols could be combined. The addition of these urban forms makes the identity more distinct, and attempts to make clear Optimo's goal of referencing the city by using "buildings, *signalétique* segments or abstract shapes that symbolize the design in the public domain." Optimo ultimately created meta-signage, a graphic language that reflects the environmental graphics of the city by *using* the environmental graphics of the city. While having a strong connection to urban signage, the resulting combinations are a step removed from the urban population, and ultimately this functionality denies the city its humanity, its essential soul.

◎◎◎◎

The bags are heavy. I take the bus home. There's a familiar-looking man sitting opposite me but I can't recall where I've seen him before. Perhaps he just reminds me of someone else I know. He's immaculately dressed, well groomed and stylish. His features are plain but honest. He has a good face, I think to myself. Then I notice a small scar on his cheek, just below his left eye, and a tattoo of Snoopy on the underside of his right wrist. Now the longer I look at him the more unfamiliar he seems.

Conor Mangat's solution is based on instinctually drawing a correlation between what he considers to be the essential personality traits of the occupants of the Twin Cities and the characteristics of his typeface. The resulting design, a single weight of upper and lower case, is overtly functional but ultimately amicable. There is a slight unevenness to the characters: the stroke width changes throughout the 'G'; there are tapered terminals at the foot of the 'i' and 'n' and the bar of the 'e'; and there are cuts into the vertex of the 'W'. The upper case is reminiscent of a tempered *Template Gothic*—the stroke is more even here—whereas the lower case has an echo of Sibylle Hagmann's *Cholla* to it. The eccentricities in Mangat's typeface (as well as those in *Template Gothic* and *Cholla*) give the typeface the depth, durability and character that Mangat was trying to achieve (SEE P. 50, 52 & 53).

As with a more traditional identity system, Mangat sees the typeface as only one component of a branding, involving choices of imagery, color and layout—he suggests these other elements could be motifs "in the grammar of location and wayfinding of proximity and place." He plays down any ostentatious quirkiness in the letterforms, instead aiming for functionality and longevity, believing the typeface should "come alive in use, where careful application accentuates its characteristics to provide continuity." A quote by Minnesotan Charles M. Schulz appears in the proposal as an appropriate adage for Mangat's perspective on the craft of type design: "I don't want to attract attention" (SEE P. 51).

By his own admission Mangat wanted to create a quiet typeface—one that "goes largely unnoticed except by one's peers" but gains prominence with use and familiarity. There's an intrinsic humility to a solution that necessitates time and patience to fully appreciate, and though a little dry on first examination, the oddities in Mangat's typeface become more apparent with closer inspection. This singular typeface is a solid and reliable workhorse that retains an approachable demeanor, and if the people of the Twin Cities share these attributes, Mangat's solution can be deemed a success.

◎◎◎◎

When I reach my house the front door is already open. I walk in. There's a man sitting in my armchair watching television, but the television is off, the screen dark. Every time he presses the remote control his face changes expression. He runs through a range of emotions, sometimes serious, sometimes comical. I put my shopping bags on the floor so I can watch him. He turns his head towards me and smiles. I smile back. He seems very friendly and I don't mind having him in my house. "Which one do you like best?" he asks me. "All of them," I reply.

LettError created a polyphonic solution comprised of a family of typefaces originally containing as many as ten to fifteen glyph variations for each particular letter. Rather than crafting a traditional font family with different weights, Erik van Blokland and Just van Rossum (LettError's "Random Twins") designed an extended family with different personalities. Instead of the 'g' gaining weight from *Roman* to *Bold*, for example, it appears with a decorative ear, or a square counter-space, or an extended or truncated tail. The entire body of glyphs has enough similarities in weight, proportion and width to be interchangeable on both a character and a typeface level, allowing the personality of the setting to range from formal to informal, quirky to corporate, functional to decorative (SEE P. 84).

The initial proposal suggested the use of a custom piece of software called LetterSetter, where complex rules behind the selection of the alternate glyphs could be hidden from the user. This would allow for context-specific glyph substitution (a certain 'e' always appearing after a 't' for example), as well as adjustment of the tone of the typeface according to exterior conditions (the form of the glyphs could change depending on the daily weather, for example). As well as this dynamic version of the typeface hosted on a special LetterSetter server, LettError intend to produce several interchangeable OpenType fonts for more general use.

The overall type design retains a sense of being personable, no matter what variant the user chooses, and remains warm and accessible and intrinsically humanist due to the lack of geometry. Many of LettError's previous typeforms (*Kosmik*, *Salmiak*, *Justlefthand* and *Erikrighthand*) have been based on handwriting and drawing, an analogue reference that is often at odds with the designers' innovative digital solutions (SEE P. 93). LettError creates typographic androids—they look and feel human, the viewer empathizes with them—but beneath the surface lurks seriously sophisticated machinery.

In their proposal, the designers claim to "blur the boundary between type designer and graphic designer." I don't think this is accurate. Instead I believe van Rossum and van Blokland empower and educate the designer who uses their typeface. They require the graphic designer to be a considered typographer, to examine closely and make a decision about every single letter in a headline. They do not ask the designer to draw any glyphs; instead they present a typographic cornucopia and encourage designers to educate themselves through their choice from among the more than seven hundred alternate shapes. Anyone interested in typography—amateur or professional—would get a thrill from using this typeface; the range of forms provides an insight into the historical richness of letterform shape. As van Blokland succinctly puts it, "Endless variation, endless discussion, something for everybody."

Technology is an integral part of the concept but, as is evident in previous LettError fonts such as *Beowolf* (SEE P. 95; SEE GLOSSARY), a random font, and *Kosmik* (SEE P. 93; SEE GLOSSARY), a flipper font, van Blokland and van Rossum do not abandon formal sophistication for modish technology. Their solution would not succeed if their drawings were not so technically accomplished. The letterforms stretch across a multitude of historical and cultural references, leaving the viewer with the impression of a rich, jumbled mass, where difference is acknowledged and where a coherent community of letterforms can sometimes overshadow variance. Rather like the individual people who make up the population of a city. As Van Blokland explains, "the style of the typeface can be changed in small, incremental steps, just as neighborhoods differ from each other and gradually change from one into the other. But it's also possible to create large contrasts between the styles. Not all combinations work well, not all alternate shapes are fit for fine typography: but that's a reflection of a large city as well."

◎◎◎◎

HABITATION

No matter how strong the concept, how well drawn the letterforms, how exciting the technology, the most important criteria for making a decision about type as a representative of a city have to be concerned with how the type "feels"—whether you can "live" with it. While all the solutions offered are successful on certain levels, at the end of the day, some "feel" better than others. Some feel like the Twin Cities. The basis for judging this can be relatively subjective since type deals with crude signifiers that are open to interpretation: we don't all "read" typefaces in the same way, we focus on dissimilar aspects, and we translate form into emotion differently. Yet sometimes there is an inexplicable affinity, when something feels intrinsically right, when an audience not versed in "reading" typography thoroughly understands what the typographic form is communicating, when the designer and the receiver connect, no matter how tenuous or subliminal that communication may be. As Caren Dewar, Deputy Regional Administrator of the Twin Cities' Metropolitan Council, stated when looking at the entrants, "I'm surprised at myself... that each typeface is creating a different reaction in me... because I never pay attention to typefaces."

LettError's proposal—selected as the winner—and the other submissions all prove it is possible to make compelling typographic forms to engage the discerning typophile and also foster interest in the typographically unaware. All the proposals reflect typography's ability to relate to a complex and wide-ranging subject, the Twin Cities. For this competition, type communicates in an appropriately vague way: it points to something while still allowing for interpretation. The joy of the "Typeface: Twin Cities" proposals is that they revel in type's heritage, playfulness and expressiveness. Such creative use of typography is a welcome breath of fresh air in an all too often predictable and gray typographic cityscape.

TYPEFACE: TWIN CITIES JURY COMMENTS & CRITIQUE

UNIVERSITY OF MINNESOTA DESIGN INSTITUTE

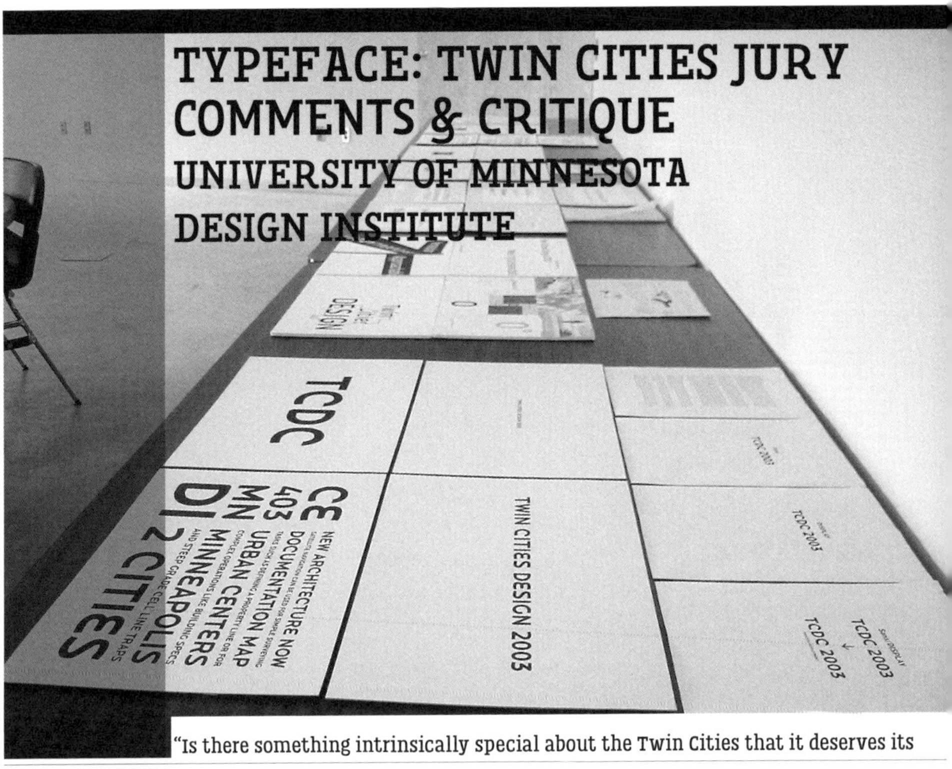

"Is there something intrinsically special about the Twin Cities that it deserves its own typeface...?"

DAY ONE: OCTOBER 16, 2002

Deborah Littlejohn: Thank you for agreeing to participate in this critique. I am delighted to be able to introduce this project to you and hear your opinions on our commission to design a typeface for the Design Institute's Twin Cities Design Celebration (TCDC). The agenda is as follows:

Take forty-five minutes to look over the submissions. Next, an hour to debate the work and comment on the projects as a whole, or make comparisons and observations between projects. Consider the intelligence of the proposals, including innovation and originality, and the relevance and appropriateness of the solutions. We'll conclude with a brief synopsis and suggestions for the projects you think have potential to be further developed.

Andrew Blauvelt: I think the problem of "local essence" is implied in the brief—"develop a typeface for the Twin Cities"—but what does that mean? Is there something intrinsically special about the Twin Cities that it deserves its own typeface or that one could generate it from those principles? That's what I'm struggling with, and I think that's what the typographers struggled with as well. Perhaps some people did better homework on the history of the Twin Cities than others, but when you look at those typefaces, that specificity is not apparent. It's the tension between the specificity of a typeface and the arbitrariness of language that typography must yield to. Eric Olson and Sybille Hagmann both get at this in their proposal descriptions.

Any of these fonts could be applied to any city. I think that folds back into the whole notion of designing an alphabet and creating a mark that was at the heart of the proposal.

nvited participants at the first day's ession held in Rapson Hall, home of the ollege of Architecture & Landscape rchitecture, included: Andrew Blauvelt, standing, far end of front table); Jan ancourt (seated, front table); Bill Moran standing, back table); Gail Swanlund standing, front table); and Carol Waldron seated, back table).

DL: And it's the next step in this commission. I think you should identify which proposals are more evocative, or have the most potential to become viable typefaces. I don't see specific visual references in these typefaces that are illustrative of the Twin Cities, and I actually think that would be kind of hokey.

AB: But it raises certain questions. The Twin Cities already have a certain duality, and how does that duality get expressed? A couple of the proposals work with this notion, but for me, there's a tension between mark-making and type-making. What if you gave the same proposal to six graphic designers instead of six type designers: what would *they* do? I'm thinking of projects like the one for Rotterdam as the 2001 Cultural Capital of Europe, which solicited proposals from five graphic design firms and asked for a systematic application to the signage, ads and literature that would be produced. How different would that be from asking a typographer to come up with a font to be used for all those same things?

Perhaps this gets a little hokey, and has a stereotyped quality, but is there a psychological profile of the Twin Cities that can be made manifest somehow? Because there really is a difference between Minneapolis and St. Paul! I've lived in both cities — I've crossed the bridges! There are different attitudes in the two cities that aren't necessarily attributable just to the architecture. The quality or pace of life is very different in both places. Maybe that could be the basis of a concept from which to generate a font. But that takes some intimate knowledge of the cities. I am glad there is one local person involved in this project, and I was curious to see how he (Eric Olson) approached the brief. It was interesting to read his proposal, because he rejects the idea of reflecting the cities' profiles, feeling that maybe it is a problem.

DL: The brief was written to serve as a springboard to generate ideas for a typeface as well as concepts for its usage. We didn't want to guide the designers too much with a very narrowly-defined program. Ultimately, this is a typeface that will be used for the Twin Cities Design Celebration, yet will hopefully connect with all kinds of people in the cities, too. We wanted to develop a really interesting typeface that progresses the field of typography and places it in the public eye in a way that people can understand — as well as being applicable for this celebration.

AB: That was the interesting thing about Peter Bilak's ["History"] proposal, which takes advantage of the TCDC event in order to talk about typography.

NEW ARCHITECTURE NO
SATELLITE NAVIGATION CAN BE USED FOR SIMPLE SURVE
DOCUMENTATION MA
TASKS SUCH AS DEFINING A PROPERTY LINE OR
URBAN CENTER
COMPLEX OPERATIONS LIKE BUILDING SP
MINNEAPOLI
AND STEEP GRADE CELL LINE TRA
2 CITIES

Eric Olson designed two companion sans serif typefaces to reflect the duality of the Twin Cities. The display version features alternate characters for some letterforms, particularly the 'E', but also the 'F', the 'C' and the 'Q'. See his proposal boards, pp. 26–28.

DL: We also saw this project as a way of encouraging a typeface that employs new uses of technology in its design or in its implementation.

AB: Overall, I found myself liking the conceptual and systematic approaches more than the formal approaches. You can tell from Peter Bilak's and LettError's proposals that they are trying to utilize the technology in a systemic way, giving it certain parameters. Which raises questions about control and about the relationship between typographer and designer.

DL: LettError addresses that relationship in their conclusion: "...[with the TCDC Alternator system] the borderline between type design and typography is blurring. The user gets more control over issues previously left to the type designer... the designer gets more control over typography."

Bill Moran: There's something about Peter Bilak's first proposal that reminds me of Art Deco signage in some of the buildings in downtown St. Paul and Minneapolis. Using technology to deliver different letterforms based on the amount of space available is a nice idea.

I think Peter's proposal is further developed than Optimo's, which is in the same vein, but Bil'ak's variable-width concept throws in a nice curveball. These two proposals are also the ones I would put side-by-side in comparison because of the amount of time the designers spent on the lowercase alphabet.

I am drawn to Conor's proposal because the letterforms pull me in, and the legibility is high. It feels more dated than LettError's, but both designers attempted similar things. I'm also intrigued by Bil'ak's "History" proposal in the way it asks people who aren't familiar with the process of type design to engage in thinking about it.

I think Sibylle's rationale is the best of the bunch. The raw materials she built her typeface from provide the foundation for how she brought the design of the letterforms together—street perspectives form the typeface and extend it into the locale. I think that is a really strong marriage.

Gail Swanlund: Sibylle's is the proposal that surprises me most. Her typefaces are challenging and idiosyncratic. It's an exciting entry in light of the Twin Cities and its appetite and appreciation for art—challenging as well as traditional or familiar. I thought Sybille's proposal came closest to being something curious, unique, and expressive and, I admit, difficult in some ways, due to its very distinctive forms.

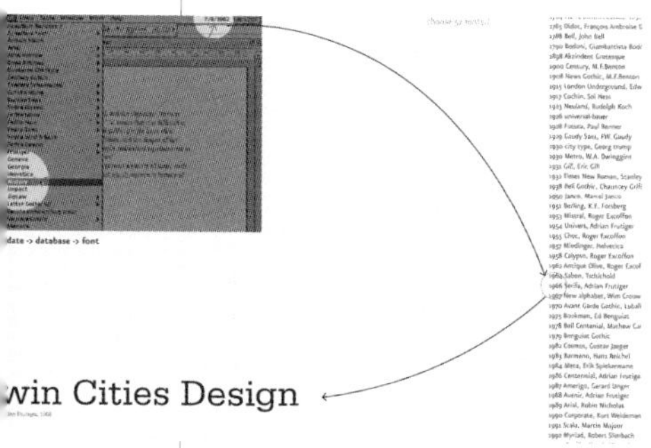

date -> database -> font

win Cities Design

eter Bil'ak's "History" proposal is ctually a computer program that ould access a database of pre-existing pefaces on the user's hard drive. The ogram would select a different typeface r each day of the year, conveying the ea that typography has a long and ried history. See his proposal boards, . 38–39.

The other proposal that is intriguing to me is Eric Olson's. This typeface has a sweetness to it—it's cute; it's "of the people." It's a populist typeface. While some aspects of the design look a little dated, it has an undeniable friendliness. It may not be the best way to think about a typeface in terms of how it would be received by Twin Citians—but in contrast to Sibylle's submission, it's highly likable and while it does have character, it is not obtrusive or extroverted. It's solid and modest and no doubt it would be easy to use.

I am also really interested in the intellectual constructs behind a few of these submissions, for example, typefaces that can be expandable and adaptable, as in LettError's and Peter Bil'ak's submissions that are delightful and surprising. I am a little bothered that Peter's typeface ends up being so blocky, and that it always must appear within a block. Could it be more suggestive of a down jacket or something really Minnesotan?

I really admire that Optimo's typeface includes the additional urban shapes. Unfortunately, the marks don't seem developed enough... They appear to be reminiscent of generic pictographs or something I have seen before—not very specific to the project. But I appreciate the idea of being able to attach them to various things, and how they might speak to the notion of personalizing. I could imagine these marks functioning as a working part of the typeface, to enhance, elaborate or identify.

Conor's typeface seems really viable to me. Like Eric Olson's, this one exudes friendliness and a bit of a sense of humor. It looks super-usable. It's approachable and vernacular. You can't help but love something that's vernacular. It's instantly lovable because of its nostalgic familiarity and honesty.

AB: Is anyone concerned that it looks like *Template Gothic*?

GS: It does have a slight resemblance.

DL: But it loses that reference on the "Twin Cities Design" board when it's typeset in two-dimensions. The slightly distorted three-dimensional rendering on the other board might remind people of Barry Deck's *Template Gothic*.

Jan Jancourt: I like Peter Bil'ak's solution of having expandable text—this elastic logotype. I just wish it could be more significant in the typestyle. The way the type fills in whatever space is available connotes the metro area in some way: we have a kind of efficiency here in the Twin Cities, we utilize every broken shoestring, it seems. I think this solution has those attributes and characteristics. And there's an elegance to it that you can't get with standard justification. The integration of technology is very effective in establishing a new way of using type. This feature will be recognizable to the broader public, too, who can appreciate the uniqueness of this technology, and also its flexibility in application.

TWIN CITIES DESIGN 2003

TWIN CITIES DESIGN 2003

TWIN CITIES DESIGN 2003

TWIN CITIES DESIGN 2003

TW CITI DESI 20

Bil'ak's first solution is an adaptable typeface that could respond to the format provided for typesetting copy. The letterforms dynamically expand and contract to fill in the available space. See his proposal boards, pp. 40–41.

DL: What about the earlier comments about the formal vocabularies being too Art Deco?

JJ: He doesn't have a complete alphabet represented, so I can't speak to that. He just came up with a typeface that was simple and generic, and that would obviously have to be developed somewhat. I'd like to see it developed with a very functional text type alongside it, or with suggestions of text that could be used in conjunction with it.

In the case of the submission by LettError, I'm a little bit concerned about how bulky the system might get, based on how many people are going to use it. One of the nice things about this proposal is that the public can marvel at it. As is, the type family has a good aesthetic sensibility—though I'm unsure whether this is the style they are actually proposing. It's a simple, dynamic concept utilizing an innovative application of technology. I hope people attending the Twin Cities Design Celebration and the wider public in the metro area would find the use of this technology interesting. It's a really strong proposal.

DL: It would be nice for people to be able to use it somehow—for example online; to typeset a logotype of their name—something simple, yet immediate.

JJ: There's going to be a lot of print collateral produced to announce the TCDC, and that might be something the public is encouraged to watch for. They'd be challenged to look at how this font changes from one application to the next.

I like that Optimo is proposing to introduce an external visual component into this alphabet, addressing some of the events planned for the TCDC itself. It could help focus people's attention; they'll be able to identify the typeface as part of the TCDC. That aspect is probably its greatest strength, but the visual elements would need to be further developed. It is somewhat generic.

Sibylle's concepts are so ambitious, yet I don't respond to the designs. The formalism has many illustrative qualities that seem too strong.

Conor offers a friendly solution, and a solid, warm, functional, sans serif font. His attribute listing consists of three words, "approachable", "vernacular" and "international." It's formally successful, and represents a serious effort. It would be flexible in use and would stand up over time, well beyond the Twin Cities Design Celebration. So would Eric Olson's, although his has somewhat retro attributes, and I think of Minneapolis in particular as being a little bit more progressive. The more I looked at these two fonts the more I liked them. Initially they seem almost too basic. They have a simple foundational core with a sophisticated level of detail and nuance that is very Midwestern. I would like this font for myself!

The formal characteristics of Conor Mangat's typeface are derived from one of the defining features of Minnesota—the weather—and universal notions of diversity, positivity and survival. See his proposal boards, pp. 50–53.

Carol Waldron: I was really intrigued with the range of Eric Olson's typeface. The display with the proposed unicase has a lot of applicability and solid qualities. I agree that the display has some dated qualities. It's quite identifiable, yet very functional. It plays to the practicality of the Twin Cities. I was intrigued by Peter Biľak's first proposal. As I evaluated them I was thinking, "how could they be applied?" With Peter Biľak's second history-based proposal, although I love the concept, I could never see the designer giving up so much control. I had a similar reaction to LettError's idea; I enjoy it very much, and I would love seeing things happen with it, but it has limited practical applicability. I really responded to the concepts and references in Optimo's and Conor's proposals. Although they don't necessarily refer to specific locale when you speak of "cities" and "the design of cities," not all typefaces here address that. It could be any city, which is a nice concept.

DL: Do you think either could refer somehow to the Twin Cities?

CW: I think there's potential for a font to capture abstractly the tenor or personalities of a place. I didn't see hybrid fonts, and I thought we might see some.

BM: That seems so difficult to me; to come up with something that specifically cites a place on a formal level. On a conceptual level, I think there's actually much more possibility.

AB: I think you could have fun with it. If it's going to be something adjusted by all the decision-making, why not push it overboard, come up with a narrative, and just twist it? For example, let's have a play about the tension between the two cities historically and contemporaneously that generates a typeface. It could be this whole melodrama, and the result could be a visible end product with this great story and a typeface to go with it. Different chapters. Different acts. It's about that kind of competition—or distinction—that the two cities seem to like to maintain.

GS: So the identifying attributes could be derived from something more like how the two cities define themselves, for example, in St. Paul's Winter Carnival and Minneapolis's Aquatennial?

AB: Yes. Winter or Summer.

T C D C

T C D C

T C D C

Gilles Gavillet and David Rust of Optimo proposed a monospaced slab serif typeface accompanied by geometric symbols that relate to urban planning and navigation systems.The letter-symbols could be used as logotypes or for wayfinding signage systems. See their proposal boards, pp. 64–65.

GS: Along that line of thinking, I think Peter Bil'ak's idea for a "Typeface of the Day" is interesting. It would be great if the end result wasn't just a static stamp on the identity of the TCDC, but something that could evolve or change...

AB: They all beg for some kind of project that presents the idea of typography to a general public, not just a typeface tha's used to brand the TCDC. That's why I was interested in Peter's "History" proposal; I thought it could be really funny. Like, "Today is such-and-such a date, and today's font is..."

DL: [laughs], *Helvetica*, flavor of the day....

AB: Like, "Today is *Baskerville*...." [laughs]

DL: But how would that change be made known? There would have to be a daily or at least weekly change. The Design Institute would constantly have to issue projects into the world...

AB: You could have this other project, a self-reflexive, "Let's Present The Typeface" project that would work around many other issues and employ a more linguistic approach. For example, is there a message-base to this city? Are there stories within this city and how might they be expressed? Or just, "The same story but in different fonts"? It seems really simple to designers, but for the public it might encourage them to be more conscious of the role typography plays in communication.

EW: Maybe it's a TCDC Journal, with entries for each day.

AB: Or you might treat the population of the city like a Type 101 class and try to explain the very basics of typography, just as in design school, when a student arrives without much prior knowledge about typography.

BM: Well, that's what's really important with the Twin Cities Design Celebration. To what extent is the public going to be involved in the project?

DL: Their participation will be crucial for the success of certain TCDC events like the Big Urban Game in September.

JJ: Does the LettError alternator system allow for different sets of parameters? Could the font reconfigure in such a way that it has, let's say, four basic gears?

DL: From what I understand, they are designing a typeface in which several alternates accompany each letter. These alternates would be combined according to context, for example, if there's an 'h' after an 'e,' then the combination is set one way. Or if the 'h' follows the 't' it would produce another configuration. Language itself provides the variables.

Twin Cities — Twin Cities Text Regular

Twin Cities — St. Paul Thin Script

Twin Cities — Minneapolis Super Bold

Twin Cities Elements

The geometries of Sibylle Hagmann's typeface are based upon perspective views defined by both cities' architecture. Her typeface comes in three weights—text, script and bold—and also features a set of decorative elements that, when combined with the letterforms, generate custom logotypes. See her proposal boards, pp. 72–75.

JJ: Let's say the font is just for Design Institute use. Would the Alternator run only in first gear, then? As it gets farther and farther out into the public realm, maybe the software would throw more variables into the mix of alternates, therefore becoming more meaningful. The resulting identity is cemented to these different types of applications. There's so much potential in this system.

EW: I wish I could see more of LettError's plans, and how it would work.

DL: Now that you all have had a chance to make comparative comments, can you now wrap things up with your specific remarks?

BM: I reacted to Peter Bil'ak's first proposal and to Conor's. My inclination would be to go back to Conor and say, "There's another step of refinement that needs to happen to see at least a consideration of historical reference."

AB: I was a little surprised at the generic quality of the symbols used in Optimo's typeface because I thought they had the potential to be more specific. I know there are only four of them represented and it's hard to imagine the rest, but I don't think they mentioned that there was any specificity attached to the marks.

I think Eric Olson's typeface is the most resolved in terms of an entire alphabet. What's disappointing is that the letterforms "TCDC" don't look terribly good together. But when I look at his other boards, the combinations of letters and the structure, it has an appeal to it in a kind of workhorse way. I like that he used the idea of duality to express the two cities.

I really like Peter's concept employing the expandable setting. This is innovative; it creates a distinctive image of the text as a whole, which is an interesting approach to take. I don't like the Art Deco-like rendering of the letterforms, but when the text block is more expanded, it has less of that feeling. I like the idea in his second proposal of trying to give some sense of history of typography to the population. It gives us an idea of what might be done with the project as a whole.

I guess I'm scared by LettError's proposal. I'm not sure what it means exactly.

Janet Abrams: You're what?

AB: Scared by it. Which may be appropriate for something about the Twin Cities. Everybody talked about how appealing to the public it would be — but is it mockery? I was joking about how it looks like Charles Schultz might have scribbled it on a pad...

JA: Have we determined that the typeface drawings on the boards are examples of what would be produced by the software mechanism?

DL: It's a rough drawing, it looks hand-lettered, though the forms would be sharpened and developed. There's the typeface, and then there's a software program called the "PanChromatic Hybrid Style Alternator"...

AB: *laughs* It's a typographic "hot dish."

GS: That's really great! So, depending on what letters are combined, the program will alter the form or the relationship between the letters. Are there also variations in each letter form — different 'a's' or 'b's' and so on?

DL: Yes: for some letters, there would be as many as ten or more alternates.

AB: Or ligatures. There's a combination.

JJ: We should assume that what we see on the boards is representative of the direction they're proposing. The ability to manipulate the font on the fly is great, and to be able to interact with how it works is also a fantastic feature. It seems you have to throw it against the wall and see what sticks.

Social quants eat justified liberties stern
Echos Erstnile Public Footpath rednecia F
danish tipografed LettError ijsje eten. E
En hard roepen hoe daar is lars en Paul. naar die luisteren natuurlijc helenaal niet. bel naar
EEFPS·aabcdeffghijjllnopnqqrst

Erik van Blokland and Just van Rossum of LettError produced a typeface with several versions for each character, whose possible combinations would be selected via computer software, called 'The PanChromatic Hybrid Style Alternator'. See their proposal boards, pp. 84–86.

JA: I am thinking about practicality as well; this font might have a lot of flexibility, but under the time pressures of putting documents together might we eventually just default to using one or two versions? I like the idea that this commission generates something special for the TCDC, but could subsequently be applied to other cities. The same process could be applied in its own way elsewhere. It sort of takes it to a meta-level. It's a new font, but it's also a new *tool*, or a version of a tool that LettError are renowned for. Whereas some of the other proposed typefaces would be more of a one-time brand, which isn't a bad thing either.

GS: How long do you expect to use this typeface?

JA: Our hope was that we would use it specifically for the materials relating to the Twin Cities Design Celebration in 2003, and possibly longer if the festival has a continued life. We'd have exclusive use of the typeface for a defined period of time.

GS: In regard to new typographic developments, I like the idea that a letterform could grow serifs, or gain weight. And while I appreciate the connection Art Deco may have historically to the Twin Cities, I am not so convinced that the Twin Cities would benefit from reviving its Art Deco roots, as suggested in Peter's typeface. With LettError's submission, I love the idea that the technology is integral to the typeface, inseparable. The typeface doesn't strike out into new territory with its form, but it is very pleasing, enthusiastic and usable. But I don't know if I could live with it for very long because it *is* just so enthusiastic!

I'm still a fan of Sibylle's typeface. It could be developed further into something very interesting. It has some Modernist-Bauhaus leanings, which I find exciting.

DL: Heritage.

GS: Yeah. The Twin Cities is the New Bauhaus. Or really, the Design Institute is the New Bauhaus.

Eric Olson's typeface feels solid, but it also seems also a little familiar to me. Maybe I'm wishing for something idiosyncratic or more specific to the Twin Cities, like having a little weather generator attached to it. But is that really necessary? The typeface has sophistication, but it also has this sincerity and workman's ethic; it goes to work, it does its job, and then it goes home. I think there's such honesty and forthrightness to his typeface that I find myself reconsidering it. I'm trying to decide if it would wear out for me too quickly. There are some things in the design that date it, some quality of the 'c's' that seems a little bit faddish.

EW: The asymmetry in the 'c's' and the curly 'e's'… I think the 'c' could be moderated a little bit and still have an asymmetrical characteristic, but gain a more comfortable balance.

BM: I found it a little bit retro, but overall, I like it. I get hung up on some individual letters. Some of them just don't seem very stable.

JJ: Eric's font is a solid design, but I do have a peeve with the fact that we're a couple of years into 2000, and we're looking back. I have the same concerns for Conor's in that it references other typefaces. Optimo's is a fairly successful solution. I can't say it any better than Andrew did; there's a generic quality to the visual marks, and there's no reason why they couldn't be more specific to this metro area. We've got a number of shapes, signs, symbols and shields that are unique and specific to this city. Whether they are all culled from the present or past or from local industry, the technology industries, the adhesive industry... I don't know. But I do see potential in Optimo's solution.

I also like LettError's concept. The one thing I have a concern over is that it has a certain hand-painted quality to it—like hand-painted signage. I don't like that connotation. I like the idea; it may be the most interesting for the spirit of the TCDC, and it could still have this warmth to it. But I'd like to see the typeface reflect the technology that's being implemented. It would be really interesting to see it harden up a bit, as is represented in some of the other panels. Hand-painting has had its day...

BM: If the aesthetic sensibilities were more refined, you might have a different conversation totally. With Peter's, the first thing I said was how much I like it, because it has this potential to fit in different contexts...

JJ: But we don't have the final typeface.

BM: Right. And I don't know that its adjustments necessarily have to happen line-for-line. It could be word-for-word. There could be scale variations within the text blocks.

JJ: The other thing that's nice about Peter's is that he's mixing letter combinations within a particular order. Even within particular words, some of the letters have a contrasting width when compared to the rest. Those variations contribute to the identity. I am really curious about the lowercase version of this font.

BM: Yes, I wonder if this system would work in lowercase. Maybe it wouldn't be as flexible.

JJ: I wonder if there's any reason why this system can't extend informally beyond the cap height or baseline and whether it's just for display only; I'm thinking of how to keep it from being so Deco-ish. How can you make this system more flexible? Maybe if one of the points in the upper-right-hand corner were lifted 15% that would keep it from being so rectangular.

GS: It's nice how the zeros start to squash when the type block is made smaller.

EW: I feel the same way... But yet, I think the letters have to be that way to work, to be able to expand and contract geometrically. I think the idea of LettError's Alternator software is intriguing. I like it very much. I just find it, um...scary. It's that usability issue.

I find Optimo's somewhat limited in terms of what we can see. The word "Twin" looks really small relative to the other words, though the softening of the geometric quality is very nice.

I wish I could see more of Conor's font. I particularly like the way it's put together in the design of the numerals. It's a nice presentation of that organic and geometric quality coming together in a typeface.

In terms of how the public would recognize a distinct quality, Eric's typeface works on the level of idiosyncrasy and as a workhorse; as a real timeless sans serif. But it doesn't have the pizzazz.

DL: Does anyone have questions or final comments before we wrap things up?

JA: Actually, there is one thing I would like to ask. Imagine these typefaces being sent to you in Belgium or Cleveland or Los Angeles, in a press release or on a poster. Which of these typefaces is going to have an impact on you if you're not here, not directly involved in the TCDC itself? Which of them might have holding-power over a year of receiving collateral material? Which one would be twinkly enough to be eye-catching the first few times, then gradually become familiar and reliable, but still resist evaporating into the fog of everybody else's branding exercises elsewhere?

The invited jury spent three hours in earnest deliberation.

I also wonder whether we're going to use other typefaces with this as a display font, and which of these will be respectful of other graphic expressions that might come up during 2003. Because we're probably not going to base all of our visual material solely on this typeface. It will be this typeface in relation to something else.

GS: In that light, I look at Eric Olson's typeface and I waffle between, "Oh, I've seen that before" and "That's really usable." And while usability is important, I will still stand up for Sibylle's proposal, which is somewhat challenging, but seems to be pushing the form. If Eric develops his typeface further, if he can bring it into 2003 without looking back, I'm still a fan of its workman-like quality. It's appropriate and honest and about the Twin Cities, though, I'm wondering if it's more St. Paul-like than Minneapolis-like!

DL: There is a lowercase that he's considering...

GS: Great idea. Could the typeface have a twin? I want it to be more contemporary, and I'd love to see it have a sibling.

AB: To present a typeface for the Twin Cities, it would be interesting not just to use it in collateral materials, but also to create a project that presents the issues of typography to a lay audience.

What's interesting about Matthew Carter's font for the Walker is that it advanced the issue of typography in creating possibilities. That's why I like Peter Biľak's proposal. It offers a possibility I haven't seen before, which could be really interesting. There's something about it that could make it an advance for the field of typography.

GS: The issue of practical control over how the LettError typeface gets used or implemented came up earlier, but I'm actually kind of excited to see what happens when a 14-year-old gets hold of a version of the LettError typeface and Alternator software. Fourteen-year-olds are really savvy, and they'll make some incredibly ugly things, but also some interesting forms. In my perfect world, I'd love to see that kind of interaction and response and involvement with the community.

DL: I think that would be the Design Institute's perfect scenario, too.

❀ ❀ ❀ ❀

DAY TWO: OCTOBER 17, 2002

Deborah Littlejohn: In our discussion yesterday we invited opinions from design professionals, critics and educators. We would also like your opinion from the point of view of a local government official working with urban design and public infrastructure.

Caren Dewar: I'm sorry I didn't get to hear the conversation, because it's by hearing the conversation that I figure out what I think.

Janet Abrams: Yesterday's group was exclusively designers and typographers, and I think they would have benefited from hearing *you*.

CD: Tell me how you picked these six designers from all over.

DL: We sent out invitations to more than just these six studios. Some of the invitees didn't respond to our invitation. There are many approaches in designing types. One approach is revivalist, making homage to existing, established fonts. Other approaches include drawing typefaces from the "ground up" with new forms, or incorporating new uses of type design technology—there was an explosion of this approach in the late Eighties and early Nineties.

For the most part, the typographers invited for the TCDC typeface commission make what are sometimes called 'original' typefaces—fonts based upon new ideas or new technologies. We wanted to commission work from young typographers who have some practical experience. And there was an idea that the typographers should have some connection to the Midwest, that they've been here before. We wanted them to have at least touched the ground.

Yesterday, we began by asking everyone, "Do you like the concept? How might it be developed further?" We read through all the proposals individually, but perhaps today we can give you a brief verbal synopsis instead. Let's go in the same order as yesterday, and look at Peter Biľak's proposals first. Peter's typeface expands and contracts to fill the space—how it looks and behaves depends upon where it is being used and how much room it is given.

JA: It could be called a Sprawl Font. *laughs* Peter also has an alternate proposal, which you're looking at now. Instead of designing a new font, he's proposing the use of pre-existing typefaces to convey the idea that typography has a long and varied history.

CD: What you're looking for is my visual reaction; I'll just ask questions along the way, if that's okay. Peter's first proposal strikes me as interesting because it relates visually to ideas in urban planning—the blocks of words look like city blocks and the different sizes of the type blocks reference how land is delegated for use.

Deputy Regional Administrator for the Twin Cities Metropolitan Council, Caren Dewar, reviewing the "Typeface: Twin Cities" proposals.

DL: Here is an entry from Erik van Blokland and Just van Rossum of LettError. Along with this typeface, they are proposing a software program that would change the combinations of a variety of its characters. We had a discussion about this proposal in yesterday's discussion, wondering if the software could also employ data from the Twin Cities. Could the physical Twin Cities influence this typeface rather than the typography capturing something about the Twin Cities?

CD: Would the public recognize that is what's happening? That the typeface is changing because of the city's data? That's very interesting...

JA: The "mutable" typeface would be online, because graphic information does not have to be static. Users could go to our website, for example, and depending upon the day or the hour, the information could reflect some calibration of Twin Cities conditions. It could essentially map them as a distortion of the font.

CD: I like the adaptability of LettError's proposal. It's very intriguing to me. It pulls me in and makes me want to see how it works. It's the mystery and the uncertainty that's appealing.

JA: The word "scared" was used twice yesterday.

ED: Was it? What I'm wrestling with in the "public official" world is that when you communicate something, people don't always receive what you've communicated in the way you intended them to. This to me represents that dilemma.

JA: But it also means that people have to come to terms with the fact that the aggregate of all the different expressions of this font may be somewhat less organized-looking than they might expect. On the other hand, that's a real representation of how diverse people's opinions are.

ED: Exactly. But I like the font itself, even without the software application. I want to touch it. However, when I look at it Peter's typeface, it's a bit cold. This is like a room, and that is not.

JA: Meaning what?

ED: The best rooms have a mix of things that pull together in some way. When I look at the LettError proposal, it's very readable. But it also has another indescribable quality to it that's drawing me in. Peter's proposal feels very industrial.

DL: The next proposal is by Gilles Gavillet and David Rust of the Swiss studio, Optimo. They are proposing to take graphic elements from urban design and maps to combine with the letterforms.

ED: It's a nice font. But their shapes remind me of a child's toy. You know, "get the round peg in the round hole."

JA: Is that a good or a bad thing?

ED: For me, the reference is not so good. The font seems simple. When I look at that font, I think of a wedding invitation.

DL: The symbols are from highways and maps. Urban planning is the reference.

ED: Which I can see from these three... That's the railroad-crossing symbol [pointing to the board].

DL: The next one is by Sibylle Hagmann. Her letterforms are based on the structure of city grids and street perspectives, and she's employing these aspects into the shapes of the letters.

ED: It's like that skyline font... It has more of an architectural feel to it. When I look at the board with the colorful logos, it still looks like the *Cityscape* typeface. It's jagged.

DL: The next one is Conor Mangat's. His idea comes from a Charles Schultz quote, "I don't want to attract attention." So he is saying that his font is...

ED: Well, that's the one we want, right!

DL: He states: "The Twin Cities are defined by their climate, a climate that, according to some, defines and characterizes their inhabitants and their attitudes." Yesterday, people described this as a "friendly, approachable typeface."

ED: It is. I think it's true. I like it. But, I would never... What do *I* know?

DL: Well, everyone has an opinion.

ED: I've never done anything like this, and I'm sitting here, surprised at myself for having reactions to these typefaces that are so different.

JA: Different than what?

ED: That each typeface is creating a different reaction in me. Because I never pay attention to typefaces.

JA: You probably do. You're just having this writ large in front of you. This is a kind of Rorschach test.

ED: I like the way the letters in Conor's typeface meet the base. I like the way they engage with the base.

DL: Do you mean there is a strong horizon?

ED: Actually, I would not say it's strong. It disappears into the base. The 'w' disappears. It softens and rounds off. It's a strong typeface that's very easy to read, but the edges of it taper off so insubstantially. And maybe that is a Charlie Brown moment. I don't know.

DL: This is Eric Olson's proposal...

ED: That upper case 'B' is very different than the one here [pointing to the board]. I look at that 'C' and I think, "something is strange with that 'C'." If you complete the circle of the 'C', you don't have a 'real' circle. And it's overreaching. Well, it's interesting. It's overreaching while at the same time it's closed.

JA: Do you want to give us a final synopsis?

ED: I love the uncertainty of the LettError proposal. I like the font itself. It's playful but also forward and the mix is interesting to me. The typeface is engaging. So if I think about a printed piece to be produced, the end result would have consistency, but also creativity. A lot can be done with it graphically. I can see the connection between the various shapes and the baseline. I can also see how maybe for some people it would be confusing.

DL: Erik and Just indicate that the font can be used very quietly. So that variation you're talking about and the flexibility, it can behave itself. And it can be rambunctious as well.

JA: And also, because we're going to be using it probably in conjunction with some other typefaces and images, there's got to be an ability for this font to be both very forward and also quite respectful of other graphic expressions that come up because of the specifics of projects. We want to have something that's consistently a characterful form, but not necessarily something that would drown out anything it appeared alongside.

ED: Well, that might be a drawback, because it's quite playful. You don't need anything else; it's a thing in itself. Conor's typeface is elegant. Again, I like the way the edges meet the base. There's a little bit of *floof!* in the lift. But LettError's proposal, it makes me smile.

GLOSSARY, TYPEFACE SAMPLER & BIOGRAPHIES

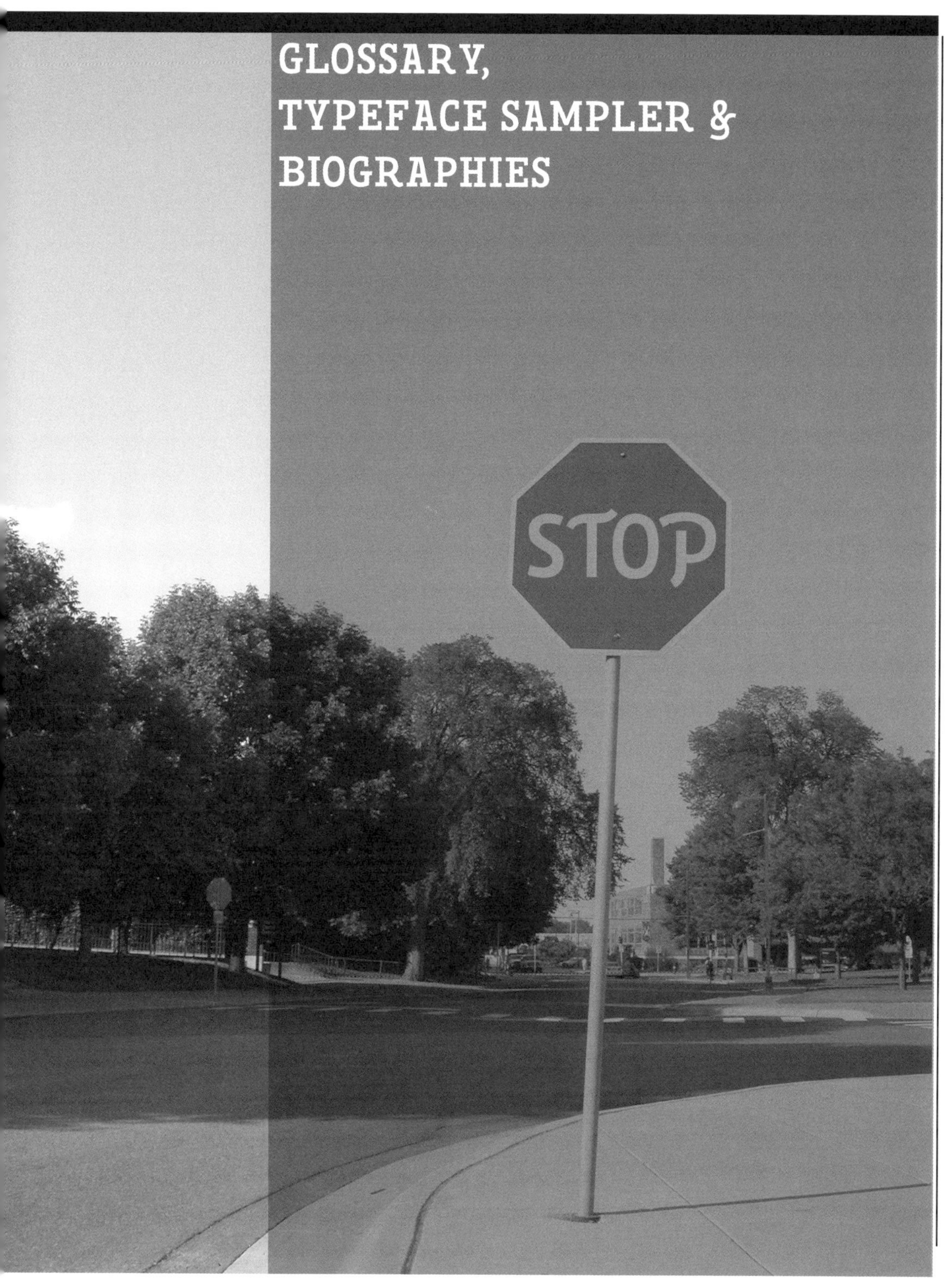

z z z z

GLYPH

A specific representation or version of a character. A font is a collection of glyphs and will often have serveral variations of a character. For instance, lowercase z, small cap z, italic z and alternate italic z.

ABCDEFGHIJKLMNOPQRST
VWXYZ 0123456789abcdfghi
*jklmnopqrstuvwxyz!@#$%^ &**
()_+¡ ™£¢∞§¶•ªº≠ “”‘’[] {} æΣ
´®†¥¨ˆøπåßƒ© ˙Δ˚ ¬…æΩ≈ ç
√∫˜µ≤≥÷/¤‹›ﬁﬂ‡°·‚—±Œ„´‰ˇÁ¨
ˆØ∏ÅÍÎÏ˝ÓÔÒÚÆ¸˛Ç◊ı˜Â¯˘¿

FONT

Originally used to refer to a collection of characters in one size and style. For instance, illustrated here, a font of nine point *Adobe Garamond Italic*. In recent years, *font* has been used to represent any number of styles or weights, related or not.

TYPEFACE

Originally a collection of fonts related in design. For instance, *Garamond*, *Garamond Italic*, *Garamond Small Caps* etc. Like *font*, the term *typeface* has suffered from confusion and is often used interchangeably with font. The two terms are now generally accepted to represent the same thing.

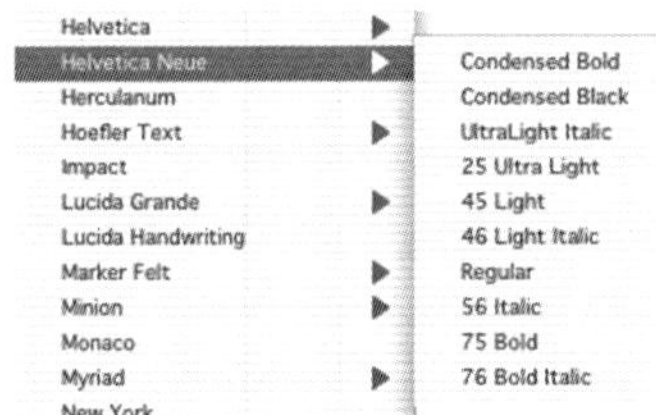

FAMILY

Used in contemporary type language to represent a group of fonts related in design. In recent years spinoff terms like ‘super family’ have been coined to better represent the robust families by designers like Luc(as) de Groot and Ole Schäfer.

Glossary ilustrations (top to bottom): Glyph, *Monotype Dante*; Font, *Adobe Garamond*; Typeface, *Adobe Garamond Roman*, *Italic* and *Small Caps*; Family, fonts provided with Apple’s OSX.

SERIF

The strokes at the beginning and or end of a letterform. The first printing types originating in the 15th century were imitations of handwriting and naturally featured serifs to mirror the entry and exit point of the pen.

BH3an*ain*
MB2an*ain*

SLAB SERIF

A typeface with large square or "slab" like serifs. These types first appeared in the early 19th century when typefounders simplified serif type designs for use within advertising.

H2EIG
HDEN6eic*na*

SANS SERIF

A letterform without serifs originating in the early 19th century when typefounders removed the serifs from slab serif designs. The type style didn't become popular, however, until almost 100 years later.

GH2Einab
DH2Einobc

MONOSPACED

A typeface whose character width is identical for each character. Originally created to accommodate the limitations imposed by typewriters and early digital devices, this space limitation has been used by designers in recent years as a form of inspiration.

one width
SAME SPACE

Serif, *Garamond 3* (top), *Minion* (bottom); Slab Serif, Digitized wood type (top), *PMN Caecilia* (bottom); Sans Serif, *Monotype Grotesque Bold Extended* (top), *DIN Mittelschrift* (bottom); Monospaced, *Platelet*.

Hx 264

LINING FIGURES

Figures sharing an equal height. Sometimes referred to as titling figures or ranging figures.

Hx 264

NON LINING FIGURES

Figures with ascenders and descenders. Sometimes referred to as old style figures, text figures or hanging figures.

Hi valentine
gas illusion
frequency

LIGATURES

Two or more letters combined into a single character to counteract the crashing effect common with combinations like "fi" and "fl". Recently, ligatures beyond those needed for legibility have emerged from their origins in calligraphy and stone cutting to be explored as new design elements. Examples include Licko's *Mrs. Eaves*, Carter's *Mantinia* and Hagmann's *Cholla*.

snuffelen en de Schifffahrt nog een
bekijken. TOEOEOET! Verdraaid, net
e laat. TAATUU!! AAARGH!?
KLABAM!? Flipperende jazzzangere

Beowolf Beowolf
Beowolf Beowolf

FLIPPER FONT

A font that cycles or "flips" through a series of defined alternates for each letter, based on its frequency of use. LettError's *FF Kosmik* is a recent example.

RANDOMFONT

A font like *FF Beowolf* that is programmed to change in printing so that no two letters are alike.

INTERPOLATION

The process made possible by digital software that allows designers to take two extreme weights (light and bold) and create intermediate weights.

Lining Figures, *Fedra Serif A*; Ligatures, *Cholla Unicase*; Flipper Font, *Kosmik* (top); Random Font, *Beowolf* (bottom); Interpolation, *Locator* in various weights.

KERNING

To reduce or enlarge the space between two forms that wouldn't normally fit together with letter spacing. Most commercially available fonts come with extensive kerning information built into the font file, minimizing the need for manual adjustment.

AT, Van
AT, Van

HINTING

Instructions within a digital font defining the vertical and horizontal stem widths to improve the display quality at low resolutions and small sizes, especially on screen. Screen-specific typefaces are often TrueType format because a more rigorous set of instructions can be built into the file than is possible with PostScript.

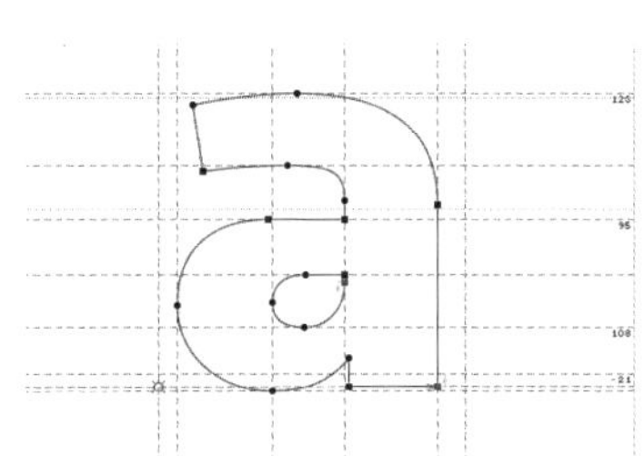

MULTIPLEMASTER

Adaptable font technology introduced by Adobe that allows users to create intermediate weights along a set of predetermined axes set by the type designer. Development for this technology has since been discontinued.

Round Square
Going Allows
Create Detroit

OPENTYPE

A new cross-platform font format (similar to current formats TrueType and PostScript) combining bitmap, metric and outline data into a single file. Built around Unicode (an international character encoding), OpenType allows users to access advanced typographic features and extended language support not inherent to fonts.

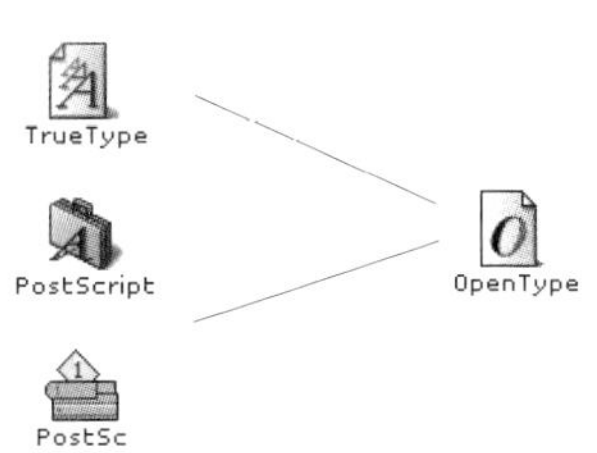

Kerning, *Locator Regular* shown with (below) and without (above) kerning; Hinting, Hints for *Locator Black*; Multiple Master, *Detroit*; OpenType, icons for the different font formats TrueType, PostScript and OpenType.

Glossary compiled and illustrated by Eric Olson.

CIRCUIT (2001)
DESIGNED BY
GILLES GAVILLET AND
DAVID RUST, OPTIMO,
SWITZERLAND.

* * * * * * * * * * *

A B C D
E F G H
I J K L M
N O P Q
R S T U
V W X Y Z

1 2 3 4 5
6 7 8 9 0
! ? ( ) / –
+ = , .

CIRCUIT IS TYPESET IN THE INTERVIEWS SECTION TO IDENTIFY SPEAKERS USING THEIR FULL NAMES AND, LATER, THEIR INITIALS.

FEDRA SERIF A (2003)
Designed by Peter Biľak,
Peter Biľak, graphic design &
typography, The Hague,
The Netherlands.

* * * * * * * * * * *

A B C D E F G H I
J K L M N O P Q R
S T U V W X Y Z
a b c d e f g h i j k
l m n o p q r s t u
v w x y z fi fl fj fï
ffi ffl ff ffj st ch
ct n fh ck
1 2 3 4 5 6 7 8 9 0 !
? ( ) / - + = , . @ #
$ % ^ & * ¡ ™ £ ¢ ∞
§ ¶ • ª º – ≠ { } " "
' ' ¿ ˘ ¯

Fedra Serif A Normal (with *Italic*, Small Caps and Expert) is typeset in the essays including: *Twin(s) it is: Birth of an Urban Font*; *Metro Letters: A Typeface for the Twin Cities*; *Marking the Place*; and *Type for the Twins: A Review of the TCDC Proposals*.

LOCATOR (2003)
Designed by Eric Olson,
Process Type Foundry,
St. Paul, MN.

* * * * * * * * * * *

A B C D E F G H I
J K L M N O P Q R S
T U V W X Y Z + **A B**
C D E F G H I J K L
M N O P Q R S T U
V W X Y Z a b c d e f
g h i j k l m n o p q r
s t u v w x y z fi fl] \
fi fl Å Æ ± µ ← → å
↑ 1 2 3 4 5 6 7 8 9 0
! ? ( ) / - + = , . @ # $
% ^ & * ¡ ™ £ ¢ ← § ¶
• ª º – { } " " ' ' ¿ ˘ ¯

Locator (with Light, Regular and **Bold** and **LOCATOR DISPLAY BOLD**) is the primary text typeface for all of the interviews as well as for the jury section and the participants' biographies.

ODILE (2003)
Designed by Sibylle Hagmann, Kontour, Houston, TX.

* * * * * * * * * * *

A B C D E F G H I
J K L M N O P Q R
S T U V W X Y Z
a b c d e f g h i j k l
m n o p q r s t u v
w x y z fi fl] \ fi fl
Å Æ ± µ å 1 2 3 4
5 6 7 8 9 0 ! ?
A B C D E F G H I J
K L M N O P Q R S
T U V W X Y Z
The Mr Mrs of Co
Inc St Blvd.

Odile Upright Italic (with Odile Special) is typeset in the Jury Comment & Critique section as well as in the typographers' interviews whenever there is a 'non-verbal' interruption in the text, eg, laughter.

PROTOCOL (2002)
Designed by Conor Mangat, Inflection, Kentfield, CA.

* * * * * * * * * * *

A B C D E F G H I
J K L M N O P Q R
S T U V W X Y Z a b
c d e f g h i j k l m n
o p q r s t u v w x y
z + *A B C D E F G H I*
J K L M N O P Q R S
T U V W X Y Z a b c d
e f g h i j k l m n o p
q r s t u v w x y z 1 2
3 4 5 6 7 8 9 0 ! ? (
) / - + = , . @ # $ & *
¡ ™ £ ¢ × § ¶ •

Protocol (with Regular and *Italic*) is typeset in all sections for the figure captions.

TWIN (2003)
Designed by Erik van Blokland and Just van Rossum, LettError, The Hague & Haarlem, The Netherlands.

* * * * * * * * * * *

A B C D E F G H I
J K L M N O P Q R
S T U V W X Y Z a b
c d e f g h i j k l m
n o p q r s t u v w x
y z + A B C D E F G H
I J K L M N O P Q R
S T U V W X Y Z a b
c d e f g h i j k l m
n o p q r s t u v w x
y z 1 2 3 4 5 6 7 8 9
0 ! ? ( ) / - + = , . @ #
$ AND ∴ ¡ ™ £ ¢ § ¶ •

Twin (here shown in a mixed edition of all ten typefaces, including BitRound, Casual, Formal, Gothic, Loopy, Sans, Poster Sans, Round, Weird, and Weird Round) is typeset in the headline titling of the chapter openers as well as the running headers and the folios.

TYPEFACE: TWIN CITIES INVITED TYPOGRAPHERS

Peter Bil'ak works in the fields of graphic, editorial, type and web design for cultural and commercial projects. He has designed several fonts for FontShop International and custom typefaces for visual identities. In 1999 he launched his online type foundry and design forum, typotheque.com. In 2000, he organized and curated an exhibition of contemporary Dutch graphic design at the Biennale of Graphic Design in Brno, Czech Republic. He is co-editor with Stuart Bailey of *Dot Dot Dot*, a graphic design and visual culture magazine that offers inventive critical journalism on topics related directly and indirectly to graphic design. He is a visiting tutor at the Royal Academy in The Hague, Art Academy in Arnhem, and regularly gives talks and workshops internationally.

Erik van Blokland and **Just van Rossum** studied at the Royal Academy for Fine & Applied Arts in The Hague. They started LettError in Berlin in 1990 with their first font, the randomizing typeface *Beowolf*. Ten years later they work on various font projects, typography, graphic design, websites and movie productions. Clients include MTV Europe, GAK (a branch of privatized government), the province of South Holland, (a branch of non-privatized government), and Apple Computer, among others. LettError's professional aspirations include computer programming of tools, design and type. The programming part is important—they've developed special applications to assist designers, such as a calendar machine for KPN, a visual noise machine for MTV, a layout-gridfitter for the PTT's (Dutch Postal Service's) Christmas stamps, map-making machines for MTV and TPG (the PTT and TNT couriers), and RoboFog, a tool for programming type designers. Other developments include BitPull, to make bitmapped type incredibly flexible, and RandomFonts and FlipperFonts to produce dynamic fonts. LettError received the Charles Nypels Award in 2000.

After finishing studies at the École Cantonale d'Art de Lausanne, **David Rust** and **Gilles Gavillet** were invited to Cranbrook Academy of Art as visiting designers. During their stay they created the MultipleMaster font *Detroit*, inspired by American advertising signage culled from studies in the Motor City. This experience led them to found Optimo in 1997. The studio's work has been exhibited mainly in its native Switzerland, including at the 1998–1999 and 2002 Swiss National Design Awards, the Basel Art Fair, and at the Museum für Gestaltung in Zürich. Rust and Gavillet have received awards for their typography from the 1999–2000 *Swiss Poster of the Year* competition, and in 2002–2003 from the *Most Beautiful Swiss Books* competition.

After earning a BFA from the Basel School of Design in 1989, **Sibylle Hagmann** worked as a designer in Switzerland. She completed her MFA at CalArts in 1996. Before relocating to Houston in 2000, she was the art director of the USC School of Architecture in Los Angeles, and taught at several southern California schools. In 1999 she completed the typeface family *Cholla* (originally commissioned by Art Center College of Design), released by *Emigre* in the same year. *Cholla* was among the winning entries in "bukva:raz!," the 2001 type design competition of the Association Typographique Internationale (ATypI). Hagmann has presented her work nationally and internationally. She currently teaches in the graphic communication program at the University of Houston.

Conor Mangat is a thirtysomething typographic designer from London. He graduated from Ravensbourne College of Design and Communication in 1991, relocating the following year to suburban Los Angeles to join the MFA program at CalArts. Graduating in 1994—and licensing his first original typeface design (*Platelet*) to *Emigre*—he went on to work at MetaDesign in San Francisco and Metro Newspapers in Silicon Valley on a variety of typo/graphic, interaction and information design projects. Returning to London in 1999, he worked independently and completed further graduate studies in typeface design at the University of Reading. In 2000, he joined Boag Associates, a specialist information design firm in London, and in 2002, returned to the San Francisco Bay Area. He is currently design director at MetaDesign.

Eric Olson is a type designer and educator living in St. Paul, Minnesota. He has produced designs for Intermedia Arts, Walker Art Center and the University of Minnesota Design Institute. In 2001 he founded Process Type Foundry as a way to showcase and market his original type designs. In addition to developing typefaces, Eric teaches type design at the Minneapolis College of Art and Design and, since February 2003, has been Assistant Design Fellow at the University of Minnesota Design Institute. He received his BFA from the University of Minnesota.

JURY & AUTHORS

Andrew Blauvelt is design director at the Walker Art Center in Minneapolis where he provides creative leadership for the design department's projects and programming. A frequent contributor to design publications and academic journals, Blauvelt writes about the history and theory of graphic design from a wider social and cultural perspective. He is the curator of *Strangely Familiar: Design and Everyday Life*, which opened at the Walker Art Center in June 2003. He has taught in the graduate program at North Carolina State University School of Design.

Caren Dewar is Deputy Regional Administrator of the Metropolitan Council, Twin Cities. She previously served as Director of the Council's Community Development Division. Prior to that she served as a Metropolitan Council Member, as Chair of both the Livable Communities Committee and of the Housing and Land Use Advisory Committee, and on the Transportation and Rail Transit Committees. Dewar has been leading and implementing comprehensive urban planning and development initiatives for 20 years. She founded Dewar and Associates, Inc. in 1996 to focus on public/private ventures that attract significant private sector participation.

Jan Jancourt studied design at Bemidji State University and received his MFA from Cranbrook Academy of Art in 1985. He then spent a year working in the Netherlands at Studio Dumbar. In 1986 he began teaching at Minneapolis College of Art and Design where he is an associate professor. He maintains an active design studio with clients that include Carleton College, American Public Radio, Hunt Adkins, Intermedia Arts, Walker Art Center and *Utne* magazine. His work has been exhibited nationally and internationally, and has been recognized by a number of publications including *Print, ID Magazine, Emigre, Idea, Critique, Design Quarterly, Dutch Graphic Design, 100 Dutch Posters, The Graphic Edge, Typography Now: The Next Wave,* and *Typography Now 2: Implosion*.

Bill Moran owns and operates Blinc Publishing, a four-person design and typography studio in historic Lowertown, St. Paul, Minnesota. As a third generation letterpress printer he is patiently crossing the wires between analog and digital technologies. Recent projects include film titling, music animation, wood typeface design and children's books. He begins teaching a new course, "Travels in Typography," at the University of Minnesota in Fall 2003, using the rare books and maps at the U's James Ford Bell Library as primary sources for studying the evolution of printing and typography.

Gail Swanlund is a native Minnesotan and designer whose professional practice includes work for art and design institutions and collaborative projects with visual artists Paul McCarthy, Benjamin Weissman and Laura Owens. Her work has been exhibited at San Francisco Museum of Modern Art, most recently in *New Acquisitions: Experimental Design*. She has been recognized by the ACD, AIGA and The Type Directors Club. Her work has been featured in *Emigre, Eye, Print, IdN* and *Zoo* as well as been published in various design anthologies including *Graphic Radicals, Radical Graphics, The Graphic Edge* and *Typographics 4*. Swanlund received her MFA from California Institute of the Arts in 1992.

Carol Waldron is an assistant professor (and currently graphic design program chair) in the Department of Design, Housing and Apparel at the University of Minnesota, in St. Paul. She teaches beginning and advanced typography, as well as color theory and bookmaking classes. She is the designer of the "Smell Map," one of the Twin Cities Knowledge Maps commissioned by the Design Institute for the Twin Cities Design Celebration. She also designed the book *Interplay: Perspectives on the Design Legacy of Jack Lenor Larsen*.

Michael Worthington is co-director of the Graphic Design program at California Institute of the Arts. His writing has been published in *Eye*, the *AIGA Journal*, *Education of a Graphic Designer*, *Sex Appeal* and *Restart: New Systems in Graphic Design*. His design work has received numerous awards, and he was the recipient of a 2001 City of Los Angeles Individual Artist Fellowship. His work has appeared in various publications and most recently was exhibited in *Californian Dream, Graphic Designers in California*, in Echirolles, France. His current practice includes writing and editorial projects, as well as graphic design and typography for print and screen. He received a BA(Hons) from Central Saint Martins School of Art and an MFA in graphic design from CalArts. He lives and works in Los Angeles.

DESIGN INSTITUTE

Janet Abrams is director of the University of Minnesota Design Institute. Raised in the era of transfer lettering, she had memorized the Letraset and Mecanorma catalogs by age 15, but got detoured into studying architecture at London University. Trained as an architectural journalist with a British trade newspaper company, she came to the U.S. as a Fulbright Scholar in 1983, moonlighted for Britain's *Blueprint* magazine, and eventually completed her PhD in architectural history at Princeton University in 1989. Her love of graphics was re-ignited as Writer-at-Large for *I.D. Magazine* in the 1990s in New York, where she diversified from architectural criticism into writing about emerging new media, and teaching in Yale's MFA graphic design program. She has programmed and co-produced several design conferences, including the AIGA's 1997 Biennial National Conference in New Orleans, Long Lake Design Camp (1996 – 99), and the 1998 Doors of Perception conference, while in Amsterdam editing *IF/THEN: Play* at the Netherlands Design Institute.

Peter Hall is the Senior Editor at the Design Institute and a contributing writer to *Metropolis* magazine. He also teaches a seminar on design theory at Yale School of Art's MFA graphic design program. He has written widely about design in its various forms, for publications including *I.D. Magazine*, *Print*, *The Guardian* and *The New York Times*. He wrote and co-edited the books *Tibor Kalman: Perverse Optimist* and *Sagmeister: Made You Look* and co-authored *Pause: 59 Minutes of Motion Graphics*.

Deborah Littlejohn has been resident Design Fellow at the University of Minnesota Design Institute since February 2002, designing and managing a variety of projects, including the DI Knowledge Maps, promotional materials and publications. She is a partner in Gusto, a St. Paul-based studio, producing print, web and interactive media for a variety of clients. Her work has been exhibited nationally and internationally, and featured in numerous publications. In 1999, Littlejohn co-curated and edited the digital design and interactive media exhibition and publication *New Genre Hybrid Language*. She has taught design, motion graphics and interactive media at several colleges in the U.S, most recently at Minneapolis College of Art and Design.

COLOPHON

Metro Letters: A Typeface for the Twin Cities is published as a document of "Typeface: Twin Cities," a component project of the Design Institute's **Twin Cities Design Celebration 2003**.

Invited typographers Eric Olson of Process Type Foundry, St. Paul, Minnesota; Peter Bil'ak of Peter Bil'ak, graphic design & typography, The Hague; Conor Mangat of Inflection, Kentfield, California; Gilles Gavillet & David Rust of Optimo, Geneva and Lausanne, Switzerland; Sibylle Hagmann of Kontour, Houston, Texas; and Erik van Blokland & Just van Rossum of LettError, Haarlem and The Hague.

Transcribed, edited and designed by Deborah Littlejohn, "Typeface: Twin Cities" Project Manager
Interviews by Janet Abrams and Deborah Littlejohn
Essays by Gail Swanlund and Michael Worthington
Editorial Consultants Janet Abrams and Peter Hall
Glossary compiled by Eric Olson. Sources: Robert Bringhurst, *The Elements of Typographic Style*, Point Roberts, WA and Vancouver, BC: Hartley & Marks, Publishers, 1992. Phil Baines and Andrew Haslam, *Type & Typography*, New York: Watson Guptill Publications, 2002.
Art and Photography for typefaces and design work are reproduced in this book courtesy of their designers. Interview photographs for Sibylle Hagmann and Conor Mangat provided by the designers; all other photos by Deborah Littlejohn. Other illustrations of design work reproduced in Gail Swanlund's and Michael Worthington's essays provided courtesy of the following studios: Andrew Blauvelt (Walker Art Center), Jonathan Hoefler (Hoefler Type Foundry), Bruce Mau (Bruce Mau Design, Inc.), Wolff Olins, Erik Spiekermann, and Rudy VanderLans (*Emigre*). Our thanks to them all.

Prepress and Printing Shapco, Inc., Minneapolis

Special Thanks to Arnie Frishman and Nancy Hoyt, Office of the General Counsel, University of Minnesota; Thomas Fisher, Dean, College of Architecture and Landscape Architecture; James Watchke, CALA Accounting; Richard Schunn, CALA Technology Director; Bonnie Lievan, University of Minnesota Foundation; Julia Fischer Baumgartner.

ISBN 0-9729696-1-6

Published by the Design Institute, University of Minnesota

UNIVERSITY OF MINNESOTA

DESIGN INSTITUTE

The Design Institute develops interdisciplinary research, educational programs and partnerships to improve design in the public realm. One of the University of Minnesota's Strategic Academic Initiatives, established with recurring funds from the Minnesota State Legislature, the Design Institute focuses on the intersections of public space, public policy and emerging media technologies. Its Fellowship program, events and publications investigate the design of products, systems and environments, as well as the underlying social processes that bring our everyday material landscape into being.

DESIGN INSTITUTE STAFF

Janet Abrams Director, TCDC Curator
Mary deLaittre TCDC General Manager
Kate Carmody Office Manager
Wendy Friedmeyer Design Minor/Design Camp Coordinator
Peter Hall Senior Editor
David Karam Digital Design Fellow
Deborah Littlejohn Design Fellow
Eric Olson Assistant Design Fellow
Alex Terzich TCDC Assistant General Manager

Design Institute
University of Minnesota
149 Nicholson Hall
216 Pillsbury Drive SE
Minneapolis, MN 55455
http://design.umn.edu
design@umn.edu

TWIN CITIES DESIGN CELEBRATION 2003

The TCDC is produced by the **Design Institute** with a generous gift from **Target Corporation**.

The TCDC comprises five related projects on mapping:
Typeface: Twin Cities — a new typeface, book and chocolates
Twin Cities Knowledge Maps — nine new cartographic interpretations of Minneapolis and St. Paul, September 2003
B.U.G. — the Big Urban Game, a massively multi-player game played in the streets of the Twin Cities, September 2003
MapCity — a new U of M Design Minor seminar on urbanism, cartography and digital technologies, Spring 2003
Else/Where: Mapping — an anthology on the political, cultural and technological implications of mapping, Spring 2004

TARGET CORPORATION

Additional funding for "Metro Letters" and a special session on "Typeface: Twin Cities" at TypeCon2003 (July 2003) has been provided by the **Mondriaan Foundation**, Amsterdam, and the **Consulate General of the Netherlands**, New York.